D0801625

The Book of Moonlight

Other books by Christopher de Vinck

The Power of the Powerless
Simple Wonders
Threads of Paradise

The Book of Moonlight

Why Life Is Good And
God Is Generous And Kind

Christopher de Vinck

ZondervanPublishingHouse
Grand Rapids, Michigan

A Division of HarperCollins*Publishers*

The Book of Moonlight
Copyright © 1998 by Christopher de Vinck

Requests for information should be addressed to:

ZondervanPublishingHouse
Grand Rapids, Michigan 49530

Library of Congress Cataloging-in-Publication Data

De Vinck, Christopher, 1951–
    The book of moonlight : why life is good and God is generous and kind /
Christopher de Vinck.
      p.   cm.
     ISBN: 0-310-21255-3 (alk. paper)
     1. De Vinck, Christopher, 1951–   —Biography. 2. Poets, American—20th
century—Biography. I. Title.
PS3554.E11588Z47   1988
277.3'082'092—dc21   97-31553
[B]   CIP

This edition printed on acid-free paper and meets the American National
Standards Institute Z39.48 standard.

All Scripture quotations, unless otherwise indicated, are taken from the *Holy
Bible: New International Version*®. NIV®. Copyright © 1973, 1978, 1984 by
International Bible Society. Used by permission of Zondervan Publishing House.
All rights reserved.

"A Halloween Transformation," "A Father's Reflection," and "Hidden Places of
the Heart" were originally printed in *The Wall Street Journal.* Reprinted by
permission of Dow Jones & Company, Inc.

*Image on pages 11, 17, 43, 67, 101 & 137 used by permission of H. Armstrong
Roberts, Inc.*

Interior design by Sue Vandenberg Koppenol

Printed in the United States of America

---

98 99 00 01 02 03 04 /❖ DC/ 10 9 8 7 6 5 4 3 2 1

To Cindy, Will,
Lynley, Lexie, and Austen

Courage! Do not stumble though the path is dark as night.
There's a star to guide the humble. Trust in God and do the right.

Edinburgh Christian Magazine,
January 1857

Contents

Waning Moon

New Jersey Moon

I look up through the trees
And see a god,
Or the eye of God,
Perhaps some artist's joke
In the night sky
Made of paint and plaster,
A first attempt to
Re-create the universe.

I step out beyond the house
And see a blue light
Against my bare arms,
These arms of alabaster.
No arms could be as weak.

I pretend to be a tree
Outstretched above the yard:
Hair spread out after
A fresh rain.

I am told no poem can be created
Outside of Paris.

I burn under this brutal light
As I walk among the trees
In this moon-filled night.

Introduction

The book of moonlight is not yet written.

Wallace Stevens (1879–1955)

This past summer I bought the moon for seven dollars and ninety-five cents. A bargain. My wife and three children and I were browsing in an international shop full of artifacts from around the world: baskets from China, brass elephants from India, glass beads from Japan, wool sweaters from Ireland. All the continents were represented, even Australia—with "genuine" boomerangs.

Just as we were about to leave the shop in search of lunch, I spotted the moon hanging on an exposed wood beam attached to the ceiling. It was one-quarter full, and it was smiling. I checked the price that dangled from its side, and then I made the purchase.

How do we place extraordinary things into our lives? How do we fit in? Ancient people believed that the moon was responsible for plant and human growth. Plutarch believed that if we are just and good our souls would be cleansed in the moon. Scientists proved that the moon affects the tides.

As the woman in the shop wrapped the moon in tissue paper, she asked me, "What do you plan to do with him?" I was not surprised that she gave the moon a gender, since we often speak about the "man in the moon." We also invite the Buffalo Girl to dance by the light of the moon.

My ten-year-old son Michael answered the saleswoman that perhaps we could eat the moon because, as he reminded us, "It's made of green cheese," but then Michael remembered that he didn't like green cheese. "It smells."

"I'll find a place for it," I weakly answered as my family and I slowly walked out of the store with the moon tucked under my arm.

We struggle each day trying to find our place in the world. In this struggle we arrange and rearrange our surroundings to enhance our homes and work space, or to make our discomfort more palatable. I didn't know where the moon was going, but I knew it was my job to find out.

I was a teenager when the first human footprint pressed against the moon's surface. Even then I remember asking myself, *What do the poets think?* The moon was once a round silk fan, or the governor of the night; the silver blanket for lovers, or the ghost-maker in October fields, but then we human beings placed a footprint in the moon dust and the moon's position was instantly rearranged in God's universe forever. How many of us have felt rearranged in our lives?

When I brought the moon home, at first I hung it in our bedroom, but my wife said it didn't match the curtains. Then I hung it in the kitchen to the left of the back door. Unfortunately, each time someone banged the door shut, the moon would bounce against the wall, rattle and shake, which, I feared, would eventually cause the moon to break in half. For two months I used the moon as a paperweight.

We, like the moon, change our faces, our moods, and our positions in the eyes of those around us, as we also seek continuity and stability. Perhaps this is why we often feel at odds with ourselves, for we human beings seek permanence while, at the same time, we dream, dance, and imagine what might be, which is the phase of our impermanence.

A few nights ago, as I wrote at my desk, as my wife and children were already sleeping, I glanced over at my pile of unanswered letters that were kept in place under my heavy, displaced moon. I walked down to the basement, fetched a nail and a hammer, then I returned to my desk. I picked up the moon and carried it out onto the deck. With a few quick blows, I struck the nail as high as I could reach into the trunk of an oak tree in my backyard, then I lifted the moon and hooked it there among the trees and darkness where it belongs.

Wallace Stevens wrote in his poem *The Comedian As the Letter C*, "The book of moonlight is not yet written." I have made my attempt to write such a book. It has been my labor these many years to capture the slow-moving light in the surrounding darkness. Among the next few pages, it is my hope that you recognize your place among the stars with your family and friends as you slowly move under the pull of a merciful God.

At times, we all drift away from God's watchful care as we try to rearrange the routines he has given us. During these times of spiritual wandering, we dream of lost possibilities and mourn the fading memories. But just as we always know where the moon is, we take comfort in the certainty that God never changes. The Psalmist sang of a mercy that endures *forever*.

The word *moon* comes from the root meaning *to measure time*. Every twenty-eight days a new moon rises. We arrange our homes and our hearts in ways that best serve those we love. This little book measures ordinary time, those small arrangements we make between the waxing and waning moon of our simple and good lives.

New

Moon

The Magic Sound

I have wandered in a face, for hours,
Passing through dark fires.
I have risen to a body
Not yet born,
Existing like a light around the body,
Through which the body moves like a sliding moon.

Robert Bly

A few winters ago I was invited to speak at a small, local, press club on why reading has declined in the United States. After the introductions, I spoke briefly about the American culture and how it seems that we, as a people, are prone to avoiding the least amount of substance in the written word; we no longer want to exert anything more beyond the mere impulse of a sensation felt from watching events on television or on the movie screen. It is easier to watch lovers kiss than to admit that we are lonely and seek solace.

I concluded my talk by comparing poetry to a crow in winter. There was this crow that accompanied me one winter morning following a formidable snowstorm. As I began to shovel the driveway, I heard a loud cawing. I looked up and saw this bird looking down at me.

A man with a shovel in winter is as congruent as a crow sitting in a tree. But, I told the audience, place the man in the tree, or hand the crow the shovel, and then you have the possibility for poetry. If you have the crow recite a favorite tale, or if you tell the man to remember how it feels to be a crow, you might hear a magic sound.

I concluded the evening's talk by saying how sad it must be for people who do not read, for they miss hearing the magic sound, and then I read aloud a few selections from my own work. The people politely applauded, and, following a poorly attended reception, I was out in the dark on the street, walking alone toward my car.

"Mr. de Vinck!" Someone called. "Mr. de Vinck, could I speak with you for a moment?"

I turned and saw through the dim lights of a distant building an old woman approaching. She extended her hand. It was warm and small.

"My name is Laura Denisovich. Denisovich like in the Solzhenitsyn book. Do you remember?"

"Yes, I remember the book."

"I read about your talk in the local paper, so I came." Laura Denisovich spoke with a Russian accent. "I wish to tell you something."

The street was draped in sheets of snow: trees like old men in drooping beards, bushes in the shape of plump, white loaves fresh from the oven; lawns filled with pillows and pancakes of snow. There was no wind.

"My grandmother, she liked to read."

I wasn't at first aware that the woman was simply following up on the lecture, for I was distracted by her face: Her right cheek was shriveled and distorted; otherwise, she was beautiful.

"When the czar was murdered, the people in my grandmother's village were told they were forbidden to read or possess books. My grandfather, he was quick to obey and began burning all the family books in the fireplace, but my grandmother, she hid Pushkin. You know Pushkin?"

I nodded yes.

"She kept his book under a loose step outside beside the porch. When my grandfather traveled on business, my grandmother would sit on the step and read aloud Pushkin's poems:

Always contented with his life
and with his dinner, and his wife."

20

I stood in the middle of a New Jersey winter, listening to old Laura Denisovich recite poetry.

Habit is heaven's own redress:
it takes the place of happiness.

"That is from his Eugene Onegin dedication poem," I said, and Laura nodded.

"It was my grandmother's most favorite poem. And when it was my time for me to learn how to read, it was from that book where I learned the shapes and sounds of the letters. They taught me how to read, my grandmother and Pushkin. I wanted to tell you this thing. And when you spoke about the crow, I was reminded of more lines my grandmother loved so well. I hadn't thought of such things for a long time until tonight:

Loved passed, the muse appeared, the weather
of mind got clarity newfound;
now free, I once more weave together
emotion, thought, and magic sound.

"Do you see, Mr. de Vinck? You spoke about the magic sound tonight. It is what I heard in my grandmother's voice when I was a child. It is what is in the crow or in the lonely man shoveling snow, right?" Laura Denisovich turned her scarred face away from the dim light. "One afternoon my grandfather returned unexpectedly from his business trip and found my grandmother reading Pushkin to me on the stoop. He raged about the czar, grabbed an ax that leaned like an innocent sailor against the house, and then my grandfather, he began to chop the steps. He pulled the book from my grandmother. She stood in silence.

"Once the steps were in a splintered pile, my grandfather lit the broken wood and tossed the book of poems into the flames. I jumped into the fire to retrieve the book. I stumbled, and my face smacked into the flames and glowing wood. I wish to tell you this. Some people, they still read. I read Pushkin, the magic sound."

Laura Denisovich asked me to autograph my book of essays, which I did, and then she said, "Please, you touch my face?"

I was embarrassed until the old women reached over, took my hand, and placed it against the rough part of her cheek. Then Laura Denisovich walked away and disappeared into the darkness, and I drove home.

We confront ourselves each day, and in such a confrontation we are challenged to believe or not to believe in the possibility of our own goodness. I think it has always been God's will that we pursue that goodness, and he has given us a soul that is capable of being filled with good or evil. Art claims that such a soul is the muse. Those who have no faith call such a soul the bank account, or the next vacation. No matter what we believe separately, we do seem to agree collectively that there is a significant option open to us as we cautiously step day to day through the field of dark shadows.

A scarecrow frightens a child. What stands out in the distance might seem, at first, to be something ugly, a half-image of an incomplete work, such as the half-built image of a man made of straw with a stick up his back; but the closer the child approaches the distortion, all that surrounds the perverted image conforms to a clear picture of a field of corn, the crows circling cautiously overhead, and the worn clothes of the farmer bleeding straw from the open sleeves. With such clarity the child is less afraid. To see truth in the light, is to deny the authority of darkness.

We cannot be afraid to choose what is righteous, to confront the darkness with our smooth hands gently placed upon a disfigured face of a woman who comes up to us in the night with the gold flames of burning poetry illuminating the scars of the powerless Devil.

Roses

Who is this that appears like the dawn,
fair as the moon, bright as the sun,
majestic as the stars in procession?

Song of Songs 6:10

If you understand the pull of sorrow and the avoidance of evil, you will understand the path toward the setting sun. In the last light of certain days, there is a reddish glow, perhaps a final bleeding that smears the low horizon—not a murder scene—but more an attempt to stop the flow that, finally, is too profuse; then all sinks into final darkness.

Much that can be found in a life can be found on the way to the dying of the light. I have always taken great solace in the recognition that we pursue comfort even though such comfort is not waiting for us in the next room, but that notion of peace, that notion of passion, that notion of an end to loneliness seems to exist inside of us just the same.

I remember Katrina, Katrina Singer, a Jewish girl, though I did not know there was such a distinction when I was a college student. To me, being born in the New Jersey suburbs, living with immigrant parents, having a blind, retarded brother, dreaming of water birds and skating with my sister, I did not know that the world divided itself from itself: Jew, Catholic, white, black, fat, skinny, poor, rich.

I disliked school, so I isolated myself from the social order that placed me at the bottom in the eyes of my peers, but at home, I was the climber of the apple trees, the boy with the raccoon hat, the son who raised robins caught in the jaws of the summer cats.

I was brought up to see that people are people with the same heart, the same dreams, the same sorrows and joys. Katrina was beautiful: black, black hair that gushed down to her shoulders, eyes of a gentle nature, skin the hue of a porcelain moon. She wore floppy hats, full sweaters, and a poise that shaped her body in a classic form of simple grace and sexuality.

I knew Katrina as a classmate at Columbia University. She was much smarter than I. Philosophy came easily to her as did statistics and history, but we were on equal terms as we read T. S. Eliot's poetry. That made all the difference.

Once in class, during our discussion on "The Love Song of J. Alfred Prufrock," Katrina turned to me and said, "I think my father was like Prufrock."

"Lonely?" I asked.

"No, insignificant in his own eyes. He was an eye doctor who often said at the dinner table, 'I don't think I will ever see as much as you, Katrina.' He was a shy man. He laughed when he made apple pies. I don't know why he liked to make such things."

In May of that year, after the exams, after the degrees were awarded, after my time in New York was complete, I had a few days to pack my clothes, collect my records of Copeland and Bach, and say good-bye to my neighbors in the dorm. During my last night I wrote a poem about old age, rolled it up, and pushed it into the belly of an empty wine bottle. I found a cork, jammed it into the tip of the bottle, then I walked out into the campus with a small garden shovel. I buried the bottle and my poem at the base of a tree, and then I covered the freshly opened earth with leaves and my dreams of one day being a writer of some worth.

The next morning I packed the car, turned in my key, and took one more walk around the campus: Law Library, Philosophy Hall, Alma Mater, the wide steps, the fountain, the days gone by caught in the memories of a school, professors, books understood and not so well-understood. At the exit gates just facing Broadway I noticed the flower vendor. He wore a cowboy hat, a shirt of silk, cut-off jeans, and sandals.

"A dozen roses for twenty," the vendor called out to no one and to everyone. "Twenty. Twenty. A dozen roses for twenty."

"I'd like to buy a flower," I said as I reached back for my wallet.

"Twenty dollars," the man said as he began to wrap the flowers in green tissue paper.

"Ah, well, no. I'd like to buy just one flower."

"One flower? You give someone a button and not the shirt? One flower no good."

The flower vendor looked at me with a smile. I smiled back. "I'd like one flower, a single rose."

"Four dollars," he said as he began to pull out the flower from the bouquet.

"But I thought you said the flowers were twenty dollars for twelve."

"That's right."

"But each rose ought to cost a little under two dollars each."

"What each," the flower vendor said. "You break up the set if you buy just one." I bought the rose for four dollars. He handed me the flower as if it were a wild onion, and he didn't give me green tissue paper.

As I turned and walked back toward the campus, I could hear above the sounds of cars honking, "Twenty-five dollars! Twenty-five dollars a dozen!"

My rose and I returned to the dorm together, walked up two flights of stairs, and stood outside Katrina's door.

I knocked. Silence. I knocked again. The door slowly opened, and there stood Katrina Singer.

"Hello, Chris," she said with a smile.

I handed her the rose, and then she stepped out into the hall and kissed my cheek, one of the best, unsolicited kisses I have ever received.

Katrina invited me into her little room. She was packing, too. We briefly spoke about our futures. She wanted to be a teacher. I didn't dare tell her about the poem in the wine bottle. I walked toward her window to take a final glimpse of the whole campus, when Katrina leaned against me to block my passage, and then she quickly reached up to grab two wet bras hanging on a thin cord near the window. She blushed. I told her that I had been offered a teaching position in a rural town in northwestern New Jersey. Katrina stuffed the bras into a suitcase, reached up to a shelf for a wine bottle, filled the bottle with water, and pierced the stem of her flower into the bottle's thin neck.

I don't remember if we shook hands, or hugged or kissed as we said good-bye, and I never saw Katrina again.

Roses are bought to speak the language of the rose, and poems are written to remember such a rose.

Often, at dusk, when the sun and clouds are placed just so, they create the color of a flower vendor's rose, and I remember how it feels to be twenty-three years old.

At times, especially when we are young, we can easily be blinded by the light, for such light fills the eyes and burns out what is necessary. The older we become, the more we understand that routine, compromise, acceptance of our ordinary place in the world are what is necessary to do what is good, and in such goodness there is sadness, sometimes regret, that we did not pursue other rays of light that broke through the tree-lined streets of our lives; but we are built to sustain such sadness.

Because we have the capacity to remember, we have the ability to arrange and rearrange our memories. If I didn't remember Katrina, she would have been a forgotten spark, a shooting star that scratched once against the dark horizon of my mind, but because of our memories, Katrina stands beside all the people I have loved; she is among the guests who often arrive in the festival of my heart, and I am able, once again, to welcome her.

When we place, side by side, who we are today with who we were yesterday, we make comparisons. It is clear that, like the moon, we reflect the light of that which glows before us: those we have loved, where we have been, and what we had once hoped to accomplish, and in such a reflection we can see a difference.

I believe that people who have been collecting bits of goodness along the way will like what they see as they pass before the mirror of eternity.

Who Am I?

God bless the moon,
And God bless me.

When do we first begin to seek a personal identity? The first time I took any particular notice of my name was in first grade, for it was in that year of 1958 that I had to learn how to spell C-H-R-I-S-T-O-P-H-E-R. I felt I was academically doomed. If my name had been John, James, or Paul, I had a fighting chance, but a name with eleven letters predetermined a lifetime of anxiety.

I was forbidden to write on my school papers simply C-H-R-I-S. "You are Christopher," my teacher announced publicly when she returned an arithmetic paper with my small, abbreviated name circled in thick, red ink. "Be proud of who you are, and don't take shortcuts." So I labored for weeks trying to learn how to spell my eleven-lettered name.

By the end of the year I had mastered the spelling of my first name, but I had not yet learned how to accept the teasing I received concerning my last name. I was, unfortunately, born with a name that rhymed with the words *fink* and *stink*, which my fellow classmates quickly discovered by the end of November.

In the spring of that year, I made a fatal error. The class was discussing genealogy and family traditions. One boy, Ben Taylor, mentioned that his parents gave him the middle name of Bernardo because his uncle was a brave man in World War II: Ben Bernardo Taylor. I never understood how Ben Taylor got away with being called by his friends *and* teachers simply Ben and not Benjamin. I had also seen plenty of his school papers and they all had the heading *Ben* Taylor, while I still had to write C-H-R-I-S-T-O-P-H-E-R.

The teacher was impressed that Ben was named after his uncle. She even added that she felt that Ben was, indeed, brave.

Then the teacher looked at the class and asked us what our middle names were. She started on one side of the classroom, and each student stated his or her middle name: Martha, John, William, Rose, Francis, Herbert, Anne, Robert. Some children had to say that they didn't have a middle name, and I genuinely felt sorry for them. I was relieved that I, for a change, could answer a teacher's question, so when it was my turn to state my middle name, I made sure I said it loudly and clearly: "Marie."

There was a pause in the classroom, a sudden hush. I waited for the next person behind me to continue with the drill, but then there was a sudden explosion of laughter that seemed to shake the picture of George Washington that watched over us throughout the year.

"Marie!" the boy next to me laughed. "That's a girl's name," then he puckered his lips and made a kissing sound. The class roared with laughter again. George Washington might have been able to save America from the British, but he would not have been any help to me on the battlefield of the first grade in St. Luke's Grammar School thirty-seven years ago.

My mother tried to reassure me that night that giving a boy the middle name of Marie was a big tradition in much of Europe. "Christopher, your father and both grandfathers all have the middle name 'Marie' as do your brothers and cousins." I wasn't impressed to the degree that even as a college student I still filled in surveys or applications with a simple M whenever I was asked to write my middle name.

I remember that in eighth grade art class we were taken to the school darkroom. No one ever learned how to develop film in that room, as far as I knew, but it was used for another one of my identity-crisis experiences.

The art teacher set up an overhead projector in that little room. One by one we took turns standing before the bright light of the projector. I remember watching the girl ahead of me. She stepped up to a place the teacher had marked on the floor. She was asked to look sideways, then, wonderfully, the girl's silhouette appeared on the cinder block wall. The teacher quickly taped a large sheet of white paper to the wall just in the right place under the girl's shadow, and then she quickly traced the girl's profile. We were asked to cut out the silhouette, write our names (our *full* names) at the bottom of the cutout, and then we were to pin it on the bulletin boards for back-to-school night.

I thought this was a great idea, so when it was my turn to step up to the marker on the floor, I stood as still as a post.

Within minutes I was sitting in the classroom, cutting out my silhouette. When it was complete, I was about to pin it to the bulletin board when a girl laughed and said, "You have such a fat head." The more I looked at my cutting, the bigger it seemed to grow. I felt grateful that I hadn't yet signed my name to the bottom. I quickly tore up my project and tossed it into the trash barrel.

As we grow older, we tend to overcome these small defeats and errors in self-judgment, but things that happened to us as children tend to haunt us in little ways throughout our lives.

I recently completed a talk in a midwestern college and was standing in line at the St. Louis International Airport. The airport was crowded and the line diminished slowly. Finally it was my turn, and I, with my bags and exhaustion, stepped up to the counter. The woman in her official uniform and serious smile flipped through my plane ticket and was about to give it an official stamp of approval when she looked at me and said, "Can I see your photo ID?"

"My what?"

"Your photo ID, sir. It's a new requirement. We have to check everyone for a photo ID."

"I haven't traveled much this year so far. I didn't know. No one told me when I flew here three days ago."

"Sir, I'm just told that unless you have a photo ID I'll have to call security, your bags will have to be X-rayed, and there's a good chance you will not be able to board the plane."

"But I'm Christopher de Vinck. My name is right on the ticket."

"But how can I be sure this is you?"

"Well, here. I have my driver's license, my credit card." I was tempted to show her how well I could spell my eleven-lettered name.

"I'm sorry, sir. Please step aside, and I'll make a call."

"Wait. I have a photo ID. I'm a writer. I happen to have one of my books in my suitcase. My picture is on the inside cover. Will that do?"

The woman looked at me. Her official smile was cracking a bit. "You're a writer?"

"Yes, here, look." I reached into my bag and pulled out my second book, *Only the Heart Knows How to Find Them*. "See. Here is my picture."

The woman looked at the picture, then she looked at me, and then her official smile broke away from her face and she offered a beautiful, genuine smile and asked, "Do you have any more books in your bag, Mr. de Vinck?"

Mr. de Vinck. I liked the sound of that name. When I became a teacher and had my first class, I stood before the children and wrote *Mr. de Vinck* on the board, and then I laughed aloud. One of my students asked me what was so funny. "Jimmy," I said, "All my life my father was Mr. de Vinck, and here I am being called Mr. de Vinck for the first time. It's just a strange feeling."

"Mr. de Vinck, do you have any more books in your bag?"

"Would you like a copy?" I asked the ticket-counter woman. She just smiled and blushed a bit. "I sure would."

I reached into my coat pocket, and grabbed my felt-tipped pen. "What is your name?"

"Josephine. My friends call me Josie, but I like my whole name."

To Josephine,
Best wishes
Christopher Marie de Vinck

Josephine upgraded my ticket to first class and I flew home.

Do you remember when Caterpillar asked Alice, "Who are you?" The poor girl was puzzled. She was tall, then short, then lost in a pool of tears. She just didn't feel like herself during most of her voyage down the rabbit hole.

In many ways we are like the lost Alice, being stretched and pulled in different directions as we travel through the dark tunnels of life, but then we see a hint of order, a sense of who we are.

If we look closely with our souls, we discover that the orderliness is God's imprint on our hearts. It is the hunger for truth and meaning that is satisfied when we accept him as father and discover our true identity.

Happy are we who can look into the mirror and see what God sees every time he looks into the heart and soul of our truest selves.

An Impulse Is Given

God made two great lights—the greater light to govern the day
and the lesser light to govern the night.

Genesis 1:16

Why do we human beings make things? Why a paper airplane? Why Picasso? Poetry? Pyramids? There are a few obvious reasons for the creative process: fame, money, beauty, but it must go beyond the obvious reasons, because there are millions of people who make things who never receive any recognition.

I think of Emily Dickinson who, once she completed a poem, placed it in her desk drawer. A farmer surely has a utilitarian purpose for stacking rocks into a wall at the far side of a field: to demonstrate boundaries, to keep the cows in, to do something with the rocks he cleared for planting, but each time I come upon an ancient rock wall and notice the care and good eye it must have taken to create the grace and the line, I can't help but wonder, What? What was the farmer thinking as he, day after day, carried these heavy rocks to their exact place? He must have stood back and admired his creation with satisfaction, knowing full well that no one would ever take notice of his labor.

Many people go through life who carry out their duties and receive no recognition. I often wish I could say thank-you to the person who planted the tree that grew the oranges, those fruit jewels that sit in my kitchen bowl. And who made the bowl?

Wasn't it true that in earlier days we could thank the baker for the extra apples in the pie, or tell the blacksmith how surefooted our horses were, or thank the carpenter for a good day's labor and see him the next day over at the church praying next to us?

Is art disconnected from the artist?

One of the first objects I created was a clay pot. When I was a child, my brother introduced me to the natural clay that accumulated in the small stream that cut through the woods of the back property. After scooping the clay from the stream bed and working out much of the moisture, I was left with a firm clump of gray earth that was transformed into a primitive clay.

One afternoon I worked a clay chunk in my hands, pushed my thumb into the middle and transformed the lump of clay into a shape that looked like a bowl. I left it on the front porch steps to dry in the afternoon sun.

The next day I retrieved my piece of art and painted red, yellow, and green stripes along the side of the bowl. To me, it looked ancient, rustic, primitive, and superb. When I offered it to my mother as a gift, she placed it on the kitchen windowsill, where it sat on display for perhaps twenty years. The best I can do to explain the creative urge is to repeat the story of that clay bowl. It is my bowl. I painted my name on the bottom.

How many times when I was a child, did I build a cabin with my Lincoln Logs and feel that deep sense of satisfaction when I topped the little house with the last piece: the red chimney block?

My father built weaving looms as a hobby and created fancy wall hangings and mohair scarves. My mother wrote poetry. I was a careful observer as a child. I watched how the robin built its nest stick by stick, mud speck by mud speck. I watched the spiders swing back and forth as they connected string to string of their new web. I liked to watch the carpenters build an addition to the neighbor's house.

Because we were a people who had to build things in order to survive, perhaps we developed this urge to continue the process. We need to build, we need to make, we need to do in order to survive. Although most of us do not exert such efforts any longer, we still have the need to create.

Each time we compose, draw, recite, dance, design, produce, we are acting out, perhaps, that survival lurch. We continue to protect ourselves. Art keeps the soul protected as a house keeps our feet warm.

Some years ago I attended a college lecture on the creative process given by a distinguished professor. Following his talk, the audience was invited to ask questions. After the typical remarks, someone stood up and asked the professor, "But why, then, does a bird sing?"

The old scholar looked up from his podium and gave a distant look beyond the audience and said "because the nest is built and the bird is not hungry."

Perhaps the best artists are those who build their nests and plant their gardens, for they are the ones who can sit beside the house while the crop grows and take a few moments to etch their names into the ground with a stick and be satisfied with such making.

We write, we compose, we create in times of rest, or in times of distress, but always in times between the building and the tearing down. Each work of art is a signature, a testimony to the time civilization has loaned us in order to step out of ourselves and re-create a portion of the universe in the face of all that cannot be recreated.

Wisdom

Even a child is known by his actions.

Proverbs 20:11

A teacher recently asked Michael, my ten-year-old son, to write down what he doesn't like, and here are his responses:

Unfairness
Meanness
People who think they
   know everything
Maura
When people moan
   and groan
People who say, "Oh,
   no, Mike is talking."
Maura
The dog when she
   jumps on me
School trips
Money
Maura
Warm pillows
My sister's face
Fleas
Bees
Moths
Bugs
Homework
Legos that constantly
   break

David playing his
   trumpet and guitar
Karen playing her
   stupid "Grease" tape
Making my bed
Cleaning my room
Doing my chores
Spiders
Geese droppings
Expensive things that
   don't work
My sister coming
   in my room
People who prove me
   wrong (which usually
   never happens)
Guns
Bombs
Knives
Wars
When light bulbs
   don't work
Spelling tests
Science tests

People who make fun
  of me
Maura
People who bother me
Some teachers
Making mistakes
Getting yelled at when
  I didn't do anything
Wet shoes in winter
Snow in my face and
  down my shirt
Maura
Sickness
People's breath
When people tell me
  what to do
Underwear
Music

Art
Gym
Bedtime
When we go for a
  lesson at the library
Being better than others
People who make fun
  of my friends
Third graders who
  throw our tennis balls
  on the roof
People who cry in class
People who copy me
Suck-ups (Maura)
People who don't want
  me to win because
  I already won

Ask a ten-year-old boy what he does not like, and he will explode from one idea to the next. Ask a tired forty-five-year-old man, and he will likely say, "Oh, the tick in the engine of my new car bothers me greatly." What happened along the way to grown-ups? We have lost God's great gift of carefreeness. We have become too smart, too sophisticated to notice who and where we are.

I remember rolling marbles on the living room carpet when I was ten. I'd squeeze a small, glass ball deep inside the space inside the crevice of my curled thumb and bent forefinger. I'd lie down flat on my stomach, take aim, adjust my hand, take aim again, and shoot. Zoom! Bam! A direct hit into the blue-and-white aggie.

I haven't played marbles in thirty-five years. I don't even remember where I left them. I used to keep them in a leather bag with a brown drawstring. They were as important to me as my car keys are important today. "You can't go through a day without your marbles," I'd say to my brother before running out of the bedroom.

Sometimes I stand out on the deck in the middle of the night, and I imagine that I can pluck the moon out of the darkness, roll it between my thumb and forefinger, and shoot it all the way across the carpet of the yard. Zoom! Bam! A direct hit into the blue-and-white earth. Flames! Explosion! A celebration of another victory, and I step back into the house and twirl my leather bag around my finger, and then I lock the door behind me and all is silent.

Do not let yourselves be dragged down by the current of life. Rise, rise above the solid earth and walk along the edge of life as if the shoreline is a single lariat, waiting for you to lasso the moon. "Do you want the moon, Mary?" George Bailey asked his buffalo girl in the film *It's a Wonderful Life*. Do you ever wonder why the Bible refers to grown-ups so many times as "children of God"? Only those who have retained the heart of a child can roll the moon, can catch the moon, can believe that the moon is for pulling down between the trees that stand over us in the middle of our good night.

Loretta Panzaroni

See the mountains kiss high heaven
And the waves clasp one another;
No sister-flowers would be forgiven
If it disdained its brother;
And the sunlight clasps the earth
And the moonbeams kiss the sea:
What are all these kissings worth
If thou kiss not me?

Love's Philosophy
Percy Bysshe Shelly

Loretta Panzaroni was the first girl I kissed.

I remember when Loretta and I took care of Mrs. Allen's chickens. Mrs. Allen, a neighbor, was the sergeant major's daughter, who married when she was nineteen. Her husband, Paul, was killed in the first month of the war while flying over England. His plane exploded, and one engine was found sixty miles away in a cornfield. The farmer thought there was a train wreck when he heard the engine smash into the earth.

Each summer Mrs. Allen spent a week at the shore with her sister and brother-in-law. The brother-in-law was a doctor, and his wife had a rose garden.

Mrs. Allen didn't particularly like chickens, except, as she often told anyone who would listen, her husband of eighteen months began the brood, built the coop, and painted it yellow with white trim, so Mrs. Allen kept collecting eggs and selling them for half the price that was charged in the markets.

Because we both knew Mrs. Allen from church, the first week of each July, Loretta and I each received an envelope in the mail requesting that we, once again, take care of the chickens. And she paid us with free eggs during the year and ten dollars each.

One particular July, a Friday, the day before Mrs. Allen was returning home from the shore, Loretta and I met in front of the yellow chicken coop and decided that we would kiss. The decision was acted upon after we entered the coop, which smelled of corn meal and hay. Loretta had a basket in her hand. It was my job to collect the eggs. We sometimes switched tasks.

I reached deep inside a brooding box, while the chickens jerked and scratched around me. The egg was white, curved, and it fit snugly in my palm. After I found another egg, I placed one in each hand. The eggs were warm and smooth. They had no blemishes. For no reason, I took one egg, closed my eyes, and slowly rolled it against my right cheek, feeling the shell brush against me. Loretta took the other egg from my hand and did the same thing.

When I opened my eyes, I watched Loretta slowly circle her cheek with the egg, and then I kissed her. Loretta Panzaroni had wet lips.

This past Thanksgiving, my wife and children and I once again returned to my parents' house for our traditional meal. My brother and sisters arrived with their families. We are all in our forties and fifties.

After the meal, my sister, my brother-in-law, and I decided to take a walk through the old neighborhood. Anne suggested that we take a look at the new development being built behind the woods along the wide field.

We tramped through bushes, against fallen leaves, over a barbed wire fence, and out toward the old Allen place that was abandoned and about to be demolished for seven condominiums.

"I wonder what happened to Mrs. Allen," I said as I looked toward the tilting chicken coop.

"She died two or three years ago," Anne answered. "She must have been in her nineties. She sold this land some time ago to developers with the stipulation that she be allowed to stay on the property for as long as she lived. She gave the money to the church."

"I'd like to take a look in the chicken coop," I said.

"What do you want to do in that old gray dump? It's about to collapse."

"Yellow."

"What?" my sister asked.

"Yellow. The chicken coop was yellow. Don't you remember, with white trim?"

"Why would anyone remember the color of a chicken coop?" Anne said as she and her husband veered off to the right toward the open field. I continued on my own toward the sagging roof.

Loretta Panzaroni painted her name and mine on the wall of the train underpass over by the newspaper store. I walked Loretta Panzaroni home from school, argued with her about the Vietnam war over the telephone, and played opposite her in the high school play, *You Can't Take It with You.*

As I stood before the old building, I could see traces of yellow paint on the clapboard. I walked up to the door, stooped down a bit, and stepped in. I remembered the vague smell of hay, the texture of the worn floor, the gray light bouncing in from the single window.

I walked up to one of the warped, gray brooding boxes and found a fragment of an old shell. I picked up the ancient piece of broken egg, closed my eyes, and swirled it against my rough face. When I opened my eyes, I almost expected to see Loretta Panzaroni.

"Chris!" my sister called from outside, from across the wide field. "Come on! We're going home!"

After I breathed in the stale air, I twirled the egg fragment in my fingers and was about to drop it into my pocket, but then I placed it back into the brooding box, rushed out into the sunlight and saw my sister and brother-in-law walking through the woods on their way home.

We live with the memory of fragments. No time or faith can ever reassemble the shattered Grecian urn to its former beauty.

Joy to the future that picks a sudden rose from yesterday's garden to be brushed against an old heart laughing. My heart is laughing, Loretta Panzaroni.

Harvest

Moon

A Halloween Transfiguration

The moon was a ghostly galleon
tossed upon cloudy seas.

Alfred Noyes

I have big ears, or so I thought when I was ten. Because I was often called Dumbo in school, I taped my ears flat to my head for a month each night before going to bed, and I even speculated how much it would hurt if I were to cut them off when I heard about Vincent Van Gogh's self-mutilation.

No one in my family knew that I harbored a secret dread for my pair of auricles that seemed to protrude from my head like radar dishes.

It was during this time of self-doubt that my fifth grade teacher read aloud Washington Irving's *The Legend of Sleepy Hollow*. I didn't understand most of the story at the time, except the part about the Galloping Hessian. He was the specter who roamed on horseback through the swamps, open glens, and mysterious hollows of Tarry Town.

I leaned forward in my desk as my teacher read the part about the goblin-rider tossing his pumpkin head at poor Ichabod Crane. That was when I decided to steal a pumpkin from the farm behind my father's woods. I had a plan.

Halloween is the time of the mask, the chance to wear a false face, to temporarily transform ourselves into someone powerful, or to heal ourselves.

I ran home under the madras skirts of the maple trees, rushed into the house, tramped up to my brother's room, and grabbed his pocket knife that I knew he kept hidden in a shoe box under his bed.

Before dinner, in that late October evening of 1961, I ran out the back door, jumped down over the five porch steps, and landed in the pile of wrinkled leaves my father had raked an hour earlier. I quickly checked to be sure that my brother's small knife hadn't fallen from my pocket; then I ran through the woods.

There is little in my memory that gave me more courage than what I felt as I entered the woods that surrounded the house where I grew up. I wanted to be free of the jeers—a strong boy with no ears.

At the far end of the woods, the neighbor's October farm stretched out like a cornucopia: apples, late corn and peppers, and a field of round pumpkins lying on their sides, prepared, it seemed, to give birth.

I crawled under the barbed wire fence, I, the hidden trespasser. I crawled on my belly until I placed a dirty hand on a ribbed, smooth pumpkin. It was the right size for my purpose, so I quickly snapped the stem from the vine, stretched my arms around the waist of the pumpkin, stood up, and ran back into my father's woods.

When I realized that no one had seen me, I sat down under a large oak tree, pulled out my brother's pocketknife, extracted the thin blade, turned the pumpkin upside down, and cut out its bottom.

Through the gaping hole, I reached in and scooped out the white seeds and orange goo until the pumpkin was hollow, then I set it upright and cut out two triangle eyes, a triangle nose, and a gap-toothed smile.

Feeling like a knight donning his suit of armor, I slowly lifted the hollow pumpkin and stuck my head through the large hole.

I was disappointed that the pumpkin didn't sit straight on my shoulders, and I had to hold it in place with my hands. I was also disappointed that the inside of a pumpkin didn't have an appealing smell; however, I was not disappointed that I felt something similar to what the first Greek actors must have felt when they slipped on their theatrical masks: different.

I was the new Galloping Hessian. I was the new, powerful, orange-headed, *earless*, goblin. I, in my masked dance, was the defender of the woods, my own Sleepy Hollow. "Woe to Ichabod Crane! Woe to those brats in school!" and then my father called me in for supper.

I lifted the mask above my head and dashed it against the thick trunk of the oak tree. "Take that!" I bellowed as I began to gallop home.

After that evening, the taunts from the school boys hurt less and less, and eventually stopped.

What we do in secret can often lead to a transfiguration.

The Geography of the Soul

Praise the Lord from the heavens,
   praise him in the heights above.
Praise him, all his angels,
   praise him, all his heavenly hosts.
Praise him, sun and moon,
   praise him, all you shining stars.

Psalm 148:1–3

I was invited to deliver a talk to the students of Greenville College in Greenville, Illinois, about faith and goodness, and about how their faith and goodness can be successfully planted in their careers and future lives.

As is the tradition in many Christian colleges, the students met in the chapel. (When I heard that I would be speaking to some students in a chapel, I thought, *How nice . . . a few students in, well, a chapel . . . those small, intimate buildings that hold perhaps thirty or forty people.*)

"Chapel" in a Christian college means CHAPEL: faculty, administrators, students. It seemed as though they had invited all of Illinois into the Greenville Chapel that warm October morning. (I thought, perhaps it was a trick, a campus tease, a midwestern play on words to call the beautiful and *large* building a chapel.)

As I was escorted to the front of the college community, I was seated with members of the staff who were going to make announcements and then introduce me. Fine. Typical. The usual procedure at a speaking engagement.

A number of students announced school business: upcoming events, changes in schedules, those who had earned special awards. I was preparing myself for my speech, easing into my position of bringing a message to the college students.

BAM! The school announcements were finished. A woman stepped to the piano. The students stood up. Silence. I looked around wondering if I should step up to the podium and begin my talk. Suddenly the music whispered a few elegant notes from the piano, then the students, all 900 of them, began to sing a song of faith.

Did you know that young people in Christian colleges sing in chapel? I didn't even know young people as a whole could sing at all. Such beauty. Such distinct voices. I stood at my place, and I listened and listened. How is this possible, such silk and power from the voices of, well, college kids? What do they know of life's struggles and victories? How could they possibly express in song what I clearly heard: struggle and victory.

After three songs, I was introduced, and then I stood before the community of young men and women, and I admitted that they ruined my talk for I had intended to be the messenger. I, in my ego, had been flown over eight hundred miles from New Jersey to Illinois to impart my words of intellect and usefulness upon the unenlightened. I think it was Greenville College's trick. They had planned this all along. The students fly in people so they can enlighten them . . . so that they can bring the message to their guests. Here I thought I was the messenger and they were the audience . . . when in God's truth I was the audience and Greenville College was the message. Clever.

On my flight home I sat beside an Air Force pilot. He flies those football-field-size C-whatever cargo planes. You've seen them. They strain the imagination with their power and dimensions.

During the beginning of our conversation, I jokingly asked if he could fly the TWA passenger jet we were sitting in, and he said, without any hesitation, that indeed he could. (*Best seat in the house*, I thought.)

As the flight progressed, the Air Force officer and I spoke about our lives, our children, our future. And then he spoke about his career, and his love of country. This man was bright, full of convictions and compassion, packaged smartly in his blue uniform. The more he spoke, the more I felt a *true* sense of protection. If men like him are in planes, command posts, ships, submarines and in Washington office buildings, well, then we are truly protected as a country and a people.

At one point the TWA captain announced that we were flying past Toronto just to the left of the plane. "And if you take a look, you'll see the Northern Lights."

I squinted out the plane window and watched blue and green sheets of light dance over the tip of the globe. The Air Force pilot leaned over, looking with me, and said in his strong voice, "I never get tired of seeing that. Beautiful."

After our plane landed in Newark, New Jersey, my Air Force pilot and I exchanged good-byes and handshakes. I wanted to give him a salute.

Finally I sat in a shuttle bus lurching toward the parking lot where I had left my car three days earlier. I was not paying much attention. The time was late evening. The exhaustion settled in. I was nodding. At one point the bus stopped. A woman stood up and walked hand-in-hand with her little boy out of the bus. Then, suddenly, she was followed by two young men carrying a collection of suitcases. I watched the four step off the bus. Nothing unusual. Then the two young men placed the bags on the curb beside the woman and small boy, then they both jumped back on the bus, returned to their seats, and closed their eyes.

So. There are college students in southern Illinois singing hymns to God, TWA pilots and United States Air Force pilots who recognize the natural beauty of the Northern Lights hovering above Toronto, Canada, and there are two strangers in Newark, New Jersey, who carry luggage for unsuspecting, grateful people.

The geography of the soul.

It Is Good to Remember

But Timothy has just now come to us from you and he has brought good news about your faith and love. He has told us that you always have pleasant memories of us and that you long to see us, just as we also long to see you.

1 Thessalonians 3:6

Insignificant memories stay with me for reasons I cannot fully explain. Are they like gold charms on a bracelet that jangle against my wrist, little trinkets that remind me of certain events or people? Are they symbols etched along the walls of the pyramid that is my mind for future interpretations or discoveries?

Many years ago when I was a teenager, my grandmother, Baba, invited me to stay with her in Brussels, Belgium. Of course, I remember the city, the relatives, the fresh strawberries Baba bought each morning, but for some reason, the memory of her sitting in the tram returns to me again and again.

One morning Baba and I received over the telephone an invitation to join my grandmother's sister for a later afternoon dinner. "We go to Tante Margaret's house," Baba announced as she swept the kitchen floor, untied her apron, and walked to the closet for her hat and coat.

"But," I asked, "didn't she invite us for three-thirty? It is so early."

"Ah," Baba smiled, "we have to walk, then take the tram, and then another tram, and then we walk some more, and then we take another tram that drops us six blocks from Tante Margaret's house."

Obviously, my grandmother and I were preparing for a long journey. I had never before been on a tram, which is another word for trolley. Brussels kept the charm and convenience of such public transportation. But it was not the tram that stays with me; it is the image of my grandmother sitting beside me as we bounced up and down along the streets of Brussels over thirty years ago.

My grandmother explained that she visited her sister at least twice a week. "She never comes to see me. She says she is too old to travel." Baba flew across the Atlantic to visit my family and me in New Jersey each year, and yet her sister felt she was too old to travel across town to visit with her sister, and Baba was *older* than Tante Margaret.

So, when I sat next to my grandmother in the city bus, I looked closely at her. She wore her long black coat and her thick-heeled, black shoes. Her black hat, probably created in the late nineteen-thirties, concealed most of her gray hair. She held her large purse on her lap as if it was going to be snatched at any moment, and she rocked back and forth with the movement of the tram. I said to myself, *She travels this route alone twice a week while I am home in the United States going to school, eating dinner, going to the movies.*

Are grandmothers supposed to be alone?

Today I might be driving to work, or walking the dog, or adjusting the pillow of my bed before I sleep when suddenly the image of my grandmother sitting in the gray bus appears, and I want once again to sit beside her.

Another image that surfaces often in my life is the red mast. One summer my father built a sailboat with a tall, red mast. For many years during our two-week vacation in Canada, my father brought the sailboat to the slow, wide river, unrolled the sails, adjusted the center board, and he was off. No matter where I was during those two weeks, I could look up and find the red mast.

My sister and I could be walking to town for chocolate ice cream and we could see through the pine trees the river, and balancing on the river's surface, the red mast. I could be on the beach, reading, and the red mast would pass by like a red pencil underlining my position on the sand.

Once, the local town merchants thought it would be good for the tourists and for business if they hired a photographer to take an aerial picture for a postcard. The man was hired; the photograph was taken, and the card was manufactured and sold in local shops. If you looked closely, you could see a small dash of red, the red mast of my father's boat right in the middle of the picture.

What hooks us to various memories? For me, perhaps, I wish to still be the boy holding my grandmother's hand on a bus, or I want to be the vacation son being unfurled and raised up along the side of the father, the strong, the core, the mast who controls the wind.

As an adult who has pursued a career in education, I am expected to guide many people. As a father I am expected to be a protector, a beacon for my own children to seek out on their way to town for their ice-cream cones. But who guides me through the city of life's puzzling streets? Baba. Who carries me up and down the river as the wind passes through my hair? My father.

Perhaps this is why God gives us the gift of unexpected, seemingly insignificant memories: to remind us that we are, indeed, still children—his children—and it is good to remember with a child's heart those who protected us, when we feel alone at night as we adjust our pillows just before we take a long breath and sleep.

Faith

Through that pure virgin shrine
That sacred veil drawn o'er Thy glorious noon,
That men might look and live, as glow-worms shine,
   And face the moon;
Wise Nicodemus saw such light
As made him know his God by night.

Henry Vaughan

One morning, a week before Christmas, as I was sitting in my room where I write, I was distracted by the slight movement of the red ribbon that hangs from the Christmas wreath out the window. There was a slight, imperceptible wind that wiggled the ribbon back and forth. *The New York Times* did not report a breeze was in the forecast.

I have always been attracted to invisible forces: wind, gravity, darkness, birds' nests. I like the coy caress of quick wind that moves through the neighborhood brushing against the rim of a Christmas wreath. Snow, rain, the human body, a flower, all succumb to the pull of gravity. Darkness conquers the house each evening, and although I have seen many nests, I have rarely seen a single bird build its home. So I was prepared for Michael's question about heaven.

That night, just after I turned out his lights for the evening, Michael yawned then said, "You know what would be the best Christmas present?"

"What would that be?" I asked my ten-year-old son.

"Well, if I knew for sure that there is a heaven."

"But Michael," I answered, "of course there's a heaven."

"How can I be sure?"

"What would you do if I said that it is snowing?"

"I'd jump out of bed and look out the window," Michael answered.

"What would you do if I said that I'm going to touch your nose?"

Michael disappeared under his blankets. "You'd have to catch it first."

"How would you know that I got your nose?"

Michael popped out from his covers and said, "I'd feel your finger."

"Right. Now Michael, wouldn't you believe me if I told you that it is snowing and we are in the basement?"

"Yeah, but I've seen snow before. I know it's real. How do you know something unless you've seen it?"

I looked at Michael's little face dimly illuminated by the small Christmas candle that stood on his windowsill. Bright boy. Innocent boy.

"If I knew for sure that there is a heaven, it would change everything."

The doubt of all humanity. The question of the ages. Wise boy. Boy of wonder.

Everything does change in a faith-filled heart.

"Daddy, do we know any old people?"

"Your grandfather is eighty-four."

"Do we know any person who is dying?"

"Why, Michael?" I asked as I adjusted his pillow.

"Well, we could ask him to send us a message and tell us that there is a heaven once he gets there."

When I was ten, I remember crying one night because I realized for the first time that my parents would someday die. At what age do we reach the age of reason, the loss of innocence?

How do we teach faith to a ten-year-old child? How do we convince a child that there is snow without his seeing the snow? How do we teach the feel of our finger against a nose when there is no finger or nose or touch of memory or night beside a father groping in the darkness for answers?

"Dad, it would be good if the dying person was from Australia."

"Why, Michael?"

"Well, he's already so far away. When he goes to heaven, he'll be far away, too, and it would be easier to believe him than someone who died in the neighborhood."

"Don't worry, Michael. There's a heaven," I said as I touched his nose. He looked up at me and smiled.

"Good night, Daddy."

"Good night, Michael."

I walked down the stairs and sat on the living room chair, picked up the newspaper and read the weather report: "Major snowstorm. Six inches by the morning."

I receive most of my information about the immediate world beyond the house from the newspaper. I receive most of my information about the not-so-immediate world from the books I read: biographies, novels, poetry collections, essays.

Children receive the most important information from their parents. I told my son not to be afraid. True answers are not found in the newspapers and in the books we read. I look carefully in the darkness. Wait for the snow. Feel the pull of life's gravity. Build nests. Believe the father. Have faith, and seek out a man from Australia. Michael wants to give him a message.

Ducks

Train a child in the way he should go, and when he is old he will not turn from it.

Proverbs 22:6

Michael, my ten-year-old son, often asks me to tell him a story, "About a time when you were a boy, something you did, Daddy." Children live in the world of immediate experiences and in the world of their dreams. They slowly grow, step by step, as they make connections between what they already know with new experiences attached to who they are.

When a father becomes a little boy in the eyes of the child, the father is like the son, and the path to maturity in the eyes of the boy seems more possible and safe. I liked telling Michael about the ducks.

One spring afternoon, my brother Bruno suggested that he, my sister, Anne, and I slip off into an adventure. I was ten, Anne was twelve, and Bruno was sixteen. "Let's go to the swamp and see if we can find duck eggs."

As I have written before, the swamp behind the house where I grew up is permanently shaped in my memory as a place that has become for me a symbol for a children's spot in heaven: this place for skating in winter and for egg hunts in the spring. The swamp was an abandoned celery farm with wide canals and narrow banks, just the right place for children to be knights in King Arthur's court, or American colonists hiding from the British.

"Let's see how many eggs we can find," Bruno suggested as the three of us walked down the steps of the back porch. Now that I look back at what I have done in my life, I see that much pleasure is drawn from anticipation. It seems that the anticipation of events can often be more thrilling than the event itself. The idea of hunting for duck eggs when you are ten years old is better than Disney World, at least it was better for me.

By the time my brother, my sister, and I stood in the middle of the swamp, we were discouraged. No duck eggs, but then there was a sudden movement in a clump of tall weeds.

"Stay here," my brother whispered. I sat down on the grass as Bruno and Anne slowly, slowly crept toward the moving brush. Suddenly Anne returned with her cupped hands extended before her.

"Sit Indian style," she called out in a hurry.

"What?" I asked.

"Sit Indian style, you silly goat!"

I sat up, crossed my legs, and waited. Anne leaned over and placed a yellow duckling inside the circle of my legs. Seconds later, Bruno returned with his offering. Back and forth they ran between me and the discovered nest. Two, four, eight, twelve ducklings in all. Each time one of the small creatures jumped over my legs, I quickly scooped it up and returned it back with the rest of the wobbling ducks.

"What were you going to do with the ducks?" Michael wanted to know as I tucked in his blanket under the mattress of his bed.

"Well, nothing. We didn't have a plan. We were looking for duck eggs, to see how many we could find. Instead, we found ducklings. Things just happened."

I want to explain to my children that in our lives things happen, that we move along with the flow of events that present themselves. These little surprises, these small stories jump up at us throughout our lives for our entertainment.

My sister and brother soon found another nest of ducklings, and they began collecting this family, too, but at one point I had to give up trying to contain all the animals and all at once they began peeping and waddling in a row down to the water's edge. "One by one," I said to Michael, "the ducks jumped into the water. I followed them. They looked like a small train on the track. When I reached the shore of the little canal, I leaned forward a bit to encourage the ducks, and then I fell in. Splash!" When I said the word *splash*, I wiggled my son's pillow and he laughed and laughed.

A few weeks after I told Michael the duck story, I returned home from work, kissed Roe and the children as they welcomed me at the door, dropped my briefcase in the dining room, hung up my coat, and walked into the kitchen.

Chicken, corn, rice, salad, water, napkins were all set on the table, prepared for the evening meal. The children waddled and wiggled to their seats. I walked to the kitchen sink to wash my hands. Steam covered the window. I looked out into the yard and saw the dim outline of the snow fort the children had built the day before, then I glanced down and there, on the window sill, were six porcelain ducks: a mother and her five offspring.

"Hey, look at the ducks!" I said.

"Michael," Roe explained, "he told me about the story, the ducks your brother and sister caught. I was in the gift store today, and I just liked these right away."

Porcelain ducks of blue and white.

"Michael, does this remind you of anything?"

"Yeah, about the ducks you found, and about the time when you fell into the swamp," he said with a smile from his seat at the dinner table.

Now our kitchen windowsill will be the narrow canal for the ducks that never left my memory.

Click. The camera takes a picture that is forever kept in the album. *Click*. A word of love is said at the right moment to a child, and that child survives the threats of anti-love in his life. *Click*. A light goes out at the end of the day, and the moon casts a dim light along the outline of my wife as she settles into bed next to me. *Click*. The heart beats again. *Click*, and again, *click*, and again. We move from story to story, from memory to memory, from day to night, and so back to the day, and we always seem to seek, like the moth, the light: the light of a father telling a story, the light of a wife, the light of a dim memory of collecting ducks on an afternoon long ago when time was young and children were yet unborn.

I reject the false memories. I reject the false fathers and mothers. I reject the neon lights that blot out the moon. I accept what is real: peace after the suffering; health after sickness; order after chaos; the flat plain after the twisted spiral; silence after the scream; silence, silence and then a song in praise of summer, wheat, water, stars, in praise of all jewels in the crown of a laughing Lord who waits for us with open arms, the Lord of my child who sleeps and dreams of ducks waddling back and forth between a father's love and a son's holy breath in the new hours of the ephemeral night.

A Father's Reflection

In a bowl to sea went wise men three
On a brilliant night in June:
They carried a net, and their hearts were set
On fishing up the moon.

Thomas Peacock (1785–1866)

When I was ten years old I discovered that beyond the front porch hundreds of "fish" swam around under the maple tree waiting to be caught. I cut a stick from the mock orange bush, found white yarn in my mother's sewing basket, and a paper clip in my father's desk. As I sat on the front steps of the house where I grew up, I tied the yarn to the tip of the stick, bent the paper clip into the shape of a hook and tied it to the end of the yarn, and then I was ready.

Casting was the most fun, sending the hook out through the air, flicking my wrist, watching how close I'd come to the intended leaf.

I was not a fisherman as a child, and I did not develop into a fisherman as an adult. I raised the small birds and rabbits our cats found in the fields. I fed a young opossum that my father found in the trash barrel one morning. Today I catch bees in a cup when they are trapped in the house, and then I free them out in the yard.

So it came as an unsettling surprise when Michael, my ten year old, asked: "Can we go fishing? Adam taught me how. Can I?" Two weeks earlier, Adam had invited Michael to join his family on a three-day camping trip.

We were on vacation, at the same cabin where I spent my vacations many years ago with my own parents along the same Canadian river two hours west of Ottawa.

I tried to hold with steady hands the summer book I was reading. Here I was in the middle of Canada, and my son wanted to split open the lip of a fish with a barbed hook.

"Michael," I said with a sense of distress in my voice, "I have an idea. Follow me." I found a stick, kite string, and a paper clip. As I began to bend the paper clip into a hook, Michael became mildly interested. When he saw that I was tying the string to the stick, and tying the hook to the string, he looked at me, and smiled. I flicked my wrist, sent the hook out under the birch tree and, on the first attempt, snagged a leaf. As I reeled in my catch, Michael quietly asked, "Dad? What are you doing?"

"Fishing."

"That isn't fishing," Michael said. "I want to go out on the river. Adam showed me how to string the pole and how to attach the hook, bobber, and bait. He also showed me how to cast. I caught three fish."

Michael is a regular chip off the old block. He loves pickles, baseball, and his mother, and so do I. But something foreign had flown from the block, a different chip, something strange.

For the first four days of the vacation, I discouraged Michael, and I finally said, "No. No fishing." By the sixth day of the vacation, Michael looked at *me* in a new way: with contempt and frustration.

"Dad," Michael pleadingly whispered in the dark on the seventh night when I adjusted his pillow. "Adam and I threw the fish back into the water. Casting is real neat." And then I remembered the sensation I felt when I cast off my own fishing line back when the maple leaves were biting.

"We'll see," I said as I kissed his forehead. I walked downstairs and rummaged in the back room of the cabin until I found the old fishing rod my brother abandoned twenty years earlier. Just as I jabbed my index finger with a hook and gave out a small cry, I noticed Michael sitting at the top of the stairs.

"Does it hurt?" Michael asked as he walked down the stairs and sat on my lap. He inspected my finger with great care.

"Nah, just stings a bit."

Michael looked at the fishing pole. "Thanks, Daddy. Adam showed me how, like this." Then my son attached the hook and placed the bobber in the appropriate place. That night, Michael slept with the fishing pole leaning against the wall beside his bed. At 6 o'clock the next morning, I heard a noise in the kitchen. I staggered through the dim, morning light.

"Adam said that bread sometimes makes good bait," Michael said, and then he pulled out a slice from a plastic bag.

Michael and I walked down to the slow-moving river. I sat down on the dock. Michael kept standing. He pressed a small piece of bread onto the hook of his pole. He flipped a small piece of metal along his reel, looped his finger in a comfortable manner, pulled his arm back, and then snapped his wrist a bit. The hook, the bait, the bobber flew up in a smooth arch above us and landed way out in the cool, morning water.

Instantly the bobber jiggled a bit. Michael gave his pole a small jerk. Again the line bounced up and down, and once again Michael gave his pole a quick pull; then the bobber disappeared and Michael's pole bent downward.

"I got one!" Michael shouted.

I stood up. "Now, play him easy. Don't lose him. Reel him in slowly," I said.

"He's a big one," Michael whooped as the line cut into the water in a zigzag manner, until the fish was visible, nearly breaking the surface, and then my son gave a final tug and the fish was up.

I watched Michael step off the dock. I watched him lean over and work the hook out of the lip of the fish. He was serious, busy, full of concentration and purpose. I looked and I looked, but I didn't see my reflection in the water below me.

I do not understand the obvious pleasure that fishing brings to millions of people, but I do understand the importance of accepting people for who they are. Michael is my son. He loves pickles, baseball, his mother, *and* fishing.

The Dance Was Lovely

Buffalo gal, won't you come out tonight,
And dance by the light of the moon?

"Buffalo Gal"
Anonymous

I cannot dance, although it is something I would like to do each morning in celebration of a day's offering. I thought about the dance for the first time when I read about the gypsies and how they danced with the bear. I, too, wanted to wander from town to town with my family safely tucked inside a brightly painted covered wagon. I wanted to sew bells to my clothes and dance with the bear. This notion of the dance is connected to my raking of the leaves.

I live in a small town that is stubbornly holding on to its attachment to the notion of an American place. There is a white church with a tall spire, the family-owned hardware store, parades, petty politics, gossip, the cemetery, proms, Santa Claus on the fire engine, the twelve o'clock whistle. Pompton Plains is a postcard photographer's dream. I live at the north end of town under seventeen oak trees. The backyard is, perhaps, one hundred feet by fifty feet, and yet there are seventeen oak trees. Enough leaves fall in my back yard to stuff all the scarecrows in America.

At the beginning of each October, I rekindle my relationship with a thin, lithe dancer. She fits in my arms with ease, is just the right height. She knows how to follow my lead, does not shy away from my hands at her waist, my partner in autumn—my bamboo rake.

For the months of October and November I walk with anticipation to the garden shed and there she is still waiting for me, tucked shyly in the corner beyond the bold wheelbarrow and the lawnmower. I reach in, and the rake seems to nearly move naturally into my waiting hand. We step out onto the leaf-covered grass and try a few tentative moves: a pulling away from each other, then a slow reunion, a near embrace. There is a natural position a man and his rake return to each fall. The more comfortable we become, the more aggressively we advance from one end of the yard to the other. The children on their bicycles ignore us. Roe looks out the living room window with approval, though my rake is less like a daughter and more like an old girlfriend: always cherished but distant and gone forever.

Do the gypsies long for a home that is not found in a single place but in the search? My rake and I have a purpose, though I'd rather that she turn into a dancer and teach me how to dance. Why do we dance with the bear? Because the bear is dangerous? Because the bear likes to dance? No, the bear is something tamed, hauled in from the wild, taken out of its place and given a new name, yet it always retains its original color and features and distant hint that it belongs someplace else, someplace exotic, cold, savage, and gentle. I believe it is the attraction to the exotic, savage, and gentle that makes us dance with the bear, the desire to *be* the bear.

Sometimes when I am sure that no one is looking, I twirl my rake around, jiggle my feet a bit in what might be considered a dance of some sort. If Gene Kelly could dance with his umbrella, well, have I got an act of equal grace!

I believe we are all meant to dance and in the intentions we create ways to move our bodies that feel right. I envy many people who can publicly rock to the rhythm of music. I think we all wish that we could cross over into the ring, raise our arms, speak a few foreign words, and command the great bear to stand, to dance, to drag his great body from one end of the circle to the other.

When my father was a young man in Belgium, he danced in all the great balls in Brussels during the 1930s and 1940s in his formal, classic tuxedo. He knew how to waltz. He spoke of those evenings with a clear memory: the polished floors, the bright lights, the dresses and flowers and music, and wide windows open for the fresh air.

For two months in the fall my rake and I make a clean sweep about every other day. Sometimes I pretend that I am in my own classic tuxedo and she curtseys before me, or I pretend I am the gypsy leading the bear, but most of the time I am just a man in a small American town raking the leaves with no recognition, no invitation. My garden clothes are ragged. My gloves have holes. And in the end, the lawn is neat and prepared for the cold winter that is surely to come, but in the coming, the dance was lovely.

Crescent

Moon

A Cup of Hot Chocolate

Everyone is a moon, and has a dark side which he never shows to anybody.

Mark Twain

Not long ago I was sitting in a hotel lounge in southern Illinois drinking a late-night cup of hot chocolate. I had delivered earlier that evening a talk on the simplicity of love in the context of being a writer and in the context of the writers I admire. I finished the speech with the notion that we all need the warm embrace of another human being to survive in peace with ourselves.

If we take much of what we consider to be classic literature, I suggested, we can see a broad picture appearing the more we read, and the more we live. What, after all, is *A Tale of Two Cities* all about, and *To Kill a Mockingbird, The Great Gatsby, Death of a Salesman, The Brothers Karamazov, The Death of Ivan Illyich, The Glass Menagerie*? Sydney Carton loved Lucy. Atticus loved his children, Scott and Jem. Gatsby loved Daisy. Willy Lowman felt that no one loved him. All the Karamazov sons suffered from the lack of love. Ivan discovered love at the very last moments of his life. And Laura—she was just waiting with hope for the gentleman caller.

It seems to me that everyone, simply, wants to be loved. After my initial words, I read excerpts from some of my books, answered a few questions, wished everyone a good night, and then I drove to my hotel.

It is my habit that after I work at my writing, which is usually in the late evening, I unwind, play a card game, reread something I wrote the week before, return to a book I liked, or I flip through the newspaper, and then I will go to bed.

When I write, there seems to be, in me, a need to cross over the river to the exotic place where passion and chaos and beauty and adventure are found with just the right combination of words strung together, and when the writing is complete for the day, I need to cross back over the running water again, back to the shore of the ordinary conditions of stability and home. That is why I wanted a cup of hot chocolate that late night in Illinois. I felt that I was still crossing over the river from the world of my writing, back to the world of home, except that home was over six hundred miles away, so a few minutes in the hotel lounge with my cup of hot chocolate would have to do.

"Are you alone tonight?" a voice drifted through the steam that rose from my cup. I looked up and saw a young woman in her twenties. Her hands were pushed into both sides of her long winter coat. Her brown knit hat was pulled down her forehead. She wore stylish leather boots. A leather purse hung from the thin strap that crossed over her right shoulder. She looked around the empty room.

"Excuse me?" I asked.

"I saw you sitting here and I thought you'd like some company." The woman had dark brown hair.

I looked around the empty room, thinking that, perhaps, the young woman had mistaken me for someone else. "Well, I guess. Would you like some hot chocolate?" She looked at me in a funny way, then shrugged her shoulders and said, "Why not?"

I was about to call the waiter, but he quickly appeared on his own. He smiled at me and welcomed the girl. "Hi, Candy. What would you like?"

"Hello, Alex."

"You know each other?" I asked. A silly question.

"Yeah," Alex the waiter said, a bit annoyed.

"I'll have a hot chocolate, like him," Candy said as she slipped out of her heavy coat.

After the waiter slid away, the girl said, "He's an old friend. He's harmless. I dated him a few times."

I am not in the habit of starting conversations with young women in the late evening hours sitting in a hotel lounge. As anyone who travels often, it is very easy to meet someone new: a person sitting beside you on a plane or train, the person standing in line at a restaurant, the person sitting beside you at a conference table, or at a workshop. People meet people when they are far from home. At first I naively thought that my meeting this women was one of those chance encounters until she said, "I'm sorry I'm late."

"Late? I don't understand," I said.

"Alex said in your note, you wrote 10:30. It's already 11:15," Candy pulled open the top of her blouse just a bit. "I'll give you an extra half-hour. It's so warm in here. I think we're sitting under a heating vent."

It was finally obvious to me that Candy was not her real name and that she was not too warm. It was not obvious to her that I had not written a note to Alex requesting a prostitute.

"I think there's been a misunderstanding," I said just as Alex reappeared with the girl's steaming hot chocolate.

"Fine. You said 10:30, and I blew it. I'll just drink this and leave if that's all you want." The young woman wrinkled her forehead a bit, then cupped the mug with her two hands.

"No, no, it's not the time. I never wrote that note to Alex."

The girl first looked around the empty room again, then she looked at me and smiled. "I suppose Alex is an idiot and I owe you an apology." She released the cup of hot chocolate and began inserting her arms into her winter coat. "This sort of thing doesn't happen so often."

"No, don't go. Could we talk?"

"Are you a policeman?" she asked.

"No, a writer."

"What do you write?" Candy asked as she once again pulled her arms out of her coat.

"Stories about myself mostly but also about people I know or meet."

She was about to leave again after she said something about newspapers and not wanting any publicity, but I convinced her that I never embarrass the people I write about and that I change the names of most people in what I write.

"Well, Candy's not my real name, anyway," she said as she took her first sip from the hot chocolate. "What do you want to talk about?"

I wanted to talk to her about the Benedictine Monks of Santo Domingo de Silos. I had just discovered their recordings and had been listening to a tape in the car on my way to the hotel. I nearly memorized the "Salve Regina," I had listened to it so often during the preceding weeks of my visit to Illinois. I didn't think Candy wanted to hear about Benedictine Monks.

"Maybe you could tell me a bit about yourself," I suggested.

"I don't have much time," Candy said as she sipped again from her cup. "So I'll tell you just one story for your next book."

"Would you mind if I took notes?" I asked.

"You won't have to. You'll remember," Candy said. After she took her third sip from her hot chocolate, she began:

It was my last night home. I'm not making this up, but I don't have time to tell you the whole story. My parents stopped sleeping in the same room by the time I was fifteen. I didn't know this for a year or so because we had an extra bedroom, a guest room attached to their room by a door. My room was down the hall a bit. I don't have any sisters or brothers. I think my mother had a miscarriage once.

So my parents stopped rocking the bed, and then they stopped talking to each other. I also knew that my father hit my mother a lot. Our house was like a cemetery. No one ever talked. I left the house early to get to school and stayed out as late as possible, mostly with friends. I'd sometimes meet new people, though.

It was easier when I got a job in a dairy store. Late hours kept me out of the house. By the time I'd come home, my mother and father were already sleeping. They never cared for me much along the way. Food was always there and clothes, and sometimes we'd go to a movie, but they never hugged each other, not that I saw, and never hugged me.

My last night, it was January six years ago. My father, he came into my room and started yelling about my boots on the living room carpet. I guess I left them on the carpet after I came home from work that night. It was late, past midnight. It was winter. Lots of snow and ice. I remember how cold it was that night because I nearly couldn't start the car after work. It was sitting in the parking lot for nearly six hours. I knew the battery was weak, and it just barely started.

My father, after he yelled about the boots, just walked up to me and slapped me in the face, my right cheek. Then he left.

I never said this to anyone, and I suppose you can write about this if you want, but I sat on my bed for about an hour, then I opened my bedroom window. I was up on the second floor. I remember the cold air gushing into the room. I reached out into the darkness and grabbed an icicle that hung down from the roof. I snapped it off and pulled in into the room. I took off my shirt and began rubbing the ice on my breast until it hurt; water ran down my body and dripped on the floor. I threw the icicle at my bedroom door, stuffed my pillowcase with a sweater, jeans, underwear, and I haven't seen my parents ever since. That was six years ago.

Candy lifted her hot chocolate one more time and drank what was left in the cup. "I gotta go," she said. "I'm supposed to meet someone after you. Any questions?"

"I don't know what to say," I weakly answered.

"I've taken care of myself. It's okay. Money doesn't replace a father, but I gotta eat and wear pretty things."

Alex stepped up to the table. "Is there anything more you want?"

Love. Peace. Acceptance. Warmth. An embrace. Compassion.

"Do you want anything else?" the waiter asked impatiently.

I looked at Candy. She checked her watch. "No, just the bill," I said.

"Well, nice talking. Thanks for the hot chocolate," Candy said as she slipped back into her coat, stood up, smiled and walked out of the lounge and disappeared. Alex looked at me with a puzzled look. "Where's she going?"

"She's just trying to keep warm, Alex. I suggest you leave her alone."

I paid my bill, took my last sip of hot chocolate, returned to my room, and went to sleep but not without a struggle.

Sometimes we get lost along the way. Before the chronometer was invented, a ship's captain could lead his crew for months at a time in a circle. Unless we have a point of reference, we cannot keep track of where we have been or where we are going. If we do not have a childhood of peace, it is difficult to know how to proceed.

I have heard from a friend who is a surgeon that so often when someone is dying, the patient calls out for his mother. We know this longing. We know the way back. Earth is the proper mother, and the moon is the wayward child revolving around and around in its own orbit but still pulling against the first waters of the oceans. We never leave the side of Eve.

If there is no place to call home, if home was a place of pain, we do attempt to replace the emptiness with a caress felt or with ornaments that dazzle us. We need artifacts of our former days and the memory of being loved, for without such history, we do not have a name. But I have met many people who have endured tragic childhoods and who have developed into people of peace and generosity, and I ask them how is it that they have overcome the loss of home, and they tell me again and again that they discovered a new childhood in the kiss of a husband and wife, or in the embrace of a son or daughter. So it is love—ultimately the love God demonstrated with the gift of his Son—that transforms the abandoned child into a new citizen of the forgiving world, the mother world, the universal embrace.

The Wild Streets of Paris

So we'll go no more a-roving
So late into the night,
Though the heart be still as loving,
And the moon be still as bright.

Lord Byron (1788–1824)

In Henry David Thoreau's book, *Walden*, he wrote this famous line: "The mass of men lead lives of quiet desperation." I believe the burden of these nine words is carried by the word *quiet*, for without that word, Thoreau would simply mean that we live in desperation, but the word *quiet* implies a decision, a choice of behavior in the face of a life filled with compromise. We live, we dream, and so we live again with memories of the dream, or with small events or trinkets that hint at what it is we have lost or desired.

The very first time I met a person who overtly shared his quiet choice was my French professor at the university.

According to the graduation requirements at the time, I was instructed to register for two years of a foreign language. Because my parents were both from Belgium, because my grandmother spent many summers with us, and because I had completed four successful years of French in high school, I signed up for French 1 in the fall of my freshman year in college. I never learned any French in school. The only reason I could speak the language at all was because my grandmother insisted that I speak with her in French. I had the vocabulary of a six-year-old Belgian child and a grandmother who loved to play cards in the kitchen.

From the first day I met my college French professor I liked him. He smiled a great deal, reassured us all that no one would fail his class, and then he subsequently didn't teach us a single thing about the French language. He told us stories about his childhood days in Paris, shared slides of his travels in Europe, and cooked us French meals on a small stove that was rigged up in the back of the classroom.

I remember his telling us that when he was a boy he lost his roller-skate key on a street in Paris. "The cobblestones had gaps between them like the spaces in my mouth," he said as he showed us the wide chasms between his teeth. The professor said "I sat in the middle of the road and wept, for the key was given to me by my grandfather along with the skates with the specific instructions to never lose the key, for, as my grandfather said, 'It is the key to the road.'" Our professor said he thought it was important to protect the key to the road.

The professor then completed his story saying that a policeman on a bicycle stopped and ran up to him to ask what the problem was. "My key," the professor said before us in class in his rich, French accent, "I've lost my key, the one to the road." The policeman summoned strangers on the street, stopped traffic, and within a few moments the key was found between two cobblestones.

At the time, I didn't think it was odd that a college French professor was telling his class about a memory such as this, and I didn't think it was strange that he shared such stories with us in English. I just liked to hear what he had to say.

In our class discussions during the year, he discovered that both my mother and father were born and raised in Belgium and met in Paris. After he learned of this, my grades in French improved.

At the end of the last day of class, the professor stopped me and suggested, "Why don't you come to my home for a good French lunch?" I accepted the invitation.

On the given day and time I appeared on the doorstep of a modest split-level house at the end of a modest road in the north-western portion of New York state. The professor's modest wife answered the door and let me in.

I remember the furniture in the house: early colonial American. The pictures on the wall were scenes of geese and railroad trains. The wife could speak only French, and the house was filled with six children under the age of twelve.

When my professor stepped out of the back bedroom, he opened his arms in welcome, gave me a gap-tooth smile, and ushered me outside to the brick patio filled with weeds.

After a delicious lunch of hamburgers on the grill and ice cream, my professor asked that his six children sing me a song, which they did: "Old MacDonald Had a Farm." I sat on a faded yellow chair made of aluminum and nylon webbing.

After the song, the children were shooed away, his wife began cleaning up the dishes, and the professor whispered, "Follow me." We walked off the patio onto a rough, untended lawn that stretched down a small slope toward a sparse measure of woods.

At the bottom of the hill, a small, quick-moving stream of clear water tumbled along. My professor smiled and asked me to stay where I was. I watched him walk toward a tree that leaned over the stream. At the base of the tree was a small, white string. The professor stooped down and began hauling in the string as if he had caught a fish. Instead of a fish, though, there was attached to the other end a round bottle of wine.

"The stream keeps it cold. It's imported from France. I thought you'd like some."

The professor uncorked the bottle, slung it up into the crook of his arm, placed the tip of the bottle to his mouth, and then he drank deeply. He offered me the bottle and I, too, taking his lead, held the bottle like an expert and drank. I returned the bottle to my professor. He corked the bottle and slowly returned it to the stream. We both watched as it slowly sank back into the water.

"Now," my professor whispered, "let me show you one more thing." He stood up straight, reached into his pocket and drew out an old key, a roller-skate key.

I didn't learn any French that year, but I learned that Thoreau was not describing all people, for there are some who just lead quiet lives among the compromises. I knew one man who knew what keys to keep: the keys to his students' minds, the key to the heart of his wife and children, the key to a cool bottle of wine, and the key to some old pair of roller skates that once belonged to a boy who flew down the wild streets of Paris.

I do not believe that God means for us to be unhappy. Sure, we despair. Sure, we have difficult times. Sure, there are degrees of loneliness and frustration and boredom. Perhaps these are signs that we just need to rest for a while. Perhaps our imperfections help us fit into the natural world that seems so precise.

We accept that we do not live in paradise. In such acceptance we need to make accommodations. A bottle of wine in a cold stream paints a picture that is different from a single bottle of wine or a single stream. Combine the two and there is an evening song with friends, toasting the rising moon, and that makes all the difference as we return to the slow routine of a Monday morning.

Shroud of Winter

There's a long, long trail a-winding
Into the land of my dreams,
Where the nightingales are singing
And a white moon beams.

Stoddard King (1889–1933)

I look out my window and see the afternoon snow. The porch rail has a collar of white, the Christmas wreath a shawl. The trees, maple in summer and old men in winter, stand like thin skeletons.

I cannot see the neighbor's shrubs. They have been transformed into large mushrooms. The hemlock to my right is a winter monster with jagged teeth and a long beard and a tall cap for boys to knock off with a single shot in their after-school travels.

What shakes down from the sky could just as well have fallen out from the glass ball my aunt sent from Belgium when I was six. Inside the ball a little man of snow prepares himself with his warm hat each time to endure the next blizzard I create with a solid shake.

The cars pass the house like slow elephants on their way in search of the next season where warmer, greener plains tend to grow.

The snow swirls upward in a sudden wind, zooms around the corner of the house in teasing anticipation of some other snow that might come around the other way.

I could just as well be in Russia and hear the bells of the sledge bounce and ring each time the horse maintains its tread with heavy hooves dropped down into the silent snow.

The postman brings a moment's color: blue uniform and yellow boots up the walk as he extends the mail to my waiting hands at the door—a green envelope—from the bank, red from the library requesting donations.

The neighborhood is a glass ball filled with cool milk up to the brim of the porch rail. The neighborhood is a green slate, covered with chalk marks and chalk dust and children zigzagging, writing their names, rolling, building forts that look more like castles made of sheep's wool.

What I see could have been created with a kitchen sponge saturated with bleach, and, using broad sweeps along the trees and grass, a whiter, paler effect might have come about, but I'd rather see the change take effect one flake at a time or a thousand times in a single afternoon out my window as I write.

There are no birds, no leaves or flowers. No grass or berries. No more road. The yard no longer has its boundaries.

In another time, a poet wrote, "Be still and know that I am God."

We can all use a bit of stillness. With the snow comes silence, unbidden. We are taken by surprise when such silence descends upon us. When I am restless, when the house seems full of noise, when the day seems to be a series of loud complaints, radio commercials, jets flying overhead, cars rolling, I like to think of the hand of my grandmother. She would bring her hand down from the darkness as she stood over my bed before I slept. I was ten. She was eighty. She'd place her hand on my head and offer a blessing in Flemish: "A cross and a sleep well," she'd whisper. How much like the silent snow, a blessing received.

Snow can silence the neighborhood as a prayer can silence a friend's anguish. I look around for my grandmother in the darkness of my bedroom sometimes just before I sleep, then the noise, the noise becomes less pronounced until there is no noise and the snow of her blessing covers me and I am *warm* and then I sleep.

Holy snow. Quiet snow. What message am I to write if I were to write such a message in the snow as children do.

As children, we wrote secret messages, or received such messages on our foreheads, and then, if we choose, we can spend the rest of our lives trying to recapture the feelings we felt when such words were created or given. I have made my choice and taken the long trip back to such snow and memory, and I have tried and tried to reproduce that feeling for my readers, for I know that the message is worth repeating.

Be still and know.

Reputation

Reputation, reputation, reputation! O! I have lost my reputation. I have lost the immortal part of myself, and what remains is bestial.

Othello, Act II, sc. iii

As a public school administrator, I had to occasionally be an arbitrator in student/teacher conflicts. One morning as I was cleaning my office, rearranging disheveled books, and filing papers, I heard, down the hallway, a loud voice. "Get out! Get out of here! You do not belong in my class!" Then there was an explosive sound as a door slammed shut.

Thinking this outburst emanated from the science wing, I didn't take much notice, for I was employed as an English department chairman, and, well, the science wing was someone else's responsibility. As I continued to clean my desk, I found an overdue book from the school library. I picked up the book, walked out of my office, and strolled down the hall toward the library, which was just around the corner.

As I turned that corner, I saw, standing beside a closed classroom door, a young boy, a freshman of oriental descent. His eyes were dark and beautifully set in an almond shape in his exquisite oval face. He stood in silence. That is when I began to make connections.

I walked up to the boy and asked him his name.

"Ly Sing."

"Ly, why are you standing in the hall?" I guessed that he was the cause of the teacher's outburst.

"Dr. de Vinck," Ly Sing began to say with sudden moisture in his eyes. "Mr. Marshall, my English teacher, he has thrown me out of his class, and I do not know where to go."

"Why did he throw you out, Ly?"

The boy looked at me. "He said I was cheating on my vocabulary quiz, and he has thrown me out of class."

"Ly, this is a serious accusation. Did you cheat?"

The boy looked down.

"I am being tutored. This is an honor's level class. I studied my words with the tutor. I knew them all, but I wasn't exactly sure about one. My notebook, it was open flat on the floor. I looked down from my paper to the open book."

Ly Sing looked at me for a response. "Ly, I have this book I need to return to the library. The class is over in a few minutes. You and I will talk with Mr. Marshall. Wait here." I walked fifteen feet, turned the corner and entered the library. The librarian smiled as I entered and offered her my late book with my apology, then she said that a few new books had arrived and perhaps I'd like to take a look. I did, indeed, want to take a look, so I stepped to the new book counter that was set against the large glass window facing the hallway.

I leaned over and was thumbing through a critical analysis of *To Kill a Mockingbird* when I suddenly felt a presence. I looked up and there was Ly Sing looking at me through the glass window, then he joined me at the counter and stood close to my side. Mr. Marshall is perhaps six feet four, and weighs perhaps two-hundred-ten pounds . . . a strong, tall, bright, loud man full of conviction and strength, and Ly Sing? Well, he was just a fourteen-year-old boy who felt that he was in deep trouble.

The bell rang. Students quickly filled the hall. "Ly, let's go to Mr. Marshall's class now and we will talk." By the time we reached the classroom, Mr. Marshall was already in the hall on his way to the principal's office.

"Mr. Marshall. I found Ly. What would you like to do?"

The teacher looked over my shoulders. "Whatever you want. We can go to the principal or we can go to your office. It doesn't matter to me."

"Let's go to my office first," I suggested.

"Fine," Mr. Marshall answered as he slung his backpack over his shoulder.

As the teacher and I walked down the hall, young Ly Sing slowly followed behind us. When we entered my office, I realized that I needed an extra chair, so while I scurried to the next room, Mr. Marshall and Ly Sing stood face-to-face waiting for my return.

Before I could roll the chair into place, Ly Sing quickly sat on my chair at my desk. I positioned my chair beside Mr. Marshall.

"Now, Ly," I said to the boy, "tell me again what happened."

He looked at me, at his teacher, and then he inhaled deeply, and slowly repeated his story about the vocabulary quiz, but this time admitting that he did, indeed, attempt to cheat.

"Ly," Mr. Marshall rumbled with authority, anger, and goodness, "It is so foolish to ruin your reputation on a stupid vocabulary quiz."

Ly Sing began to cry.

"Don't start with the tears," Mr. Marshall snapped. Ly wiped his eyes again and again.

"Don't you understand that I would much rather you turn in an honest failing grade than a cheating one? You won't understand this now, but in twenty years, Ly, you will remember this moment and you will thank your old, ugly English teacher. Don't you know that in a second, like this (Mr. Marshall snapped his fingers), you can ruin your reputation by making a single, wrong error in judgment?" Ly Sing began to cry again.

The boy looked up in my direction. "I've never cheated before," Ly Sing said to me in a pleading voice. Mr. Marshall wanted to permanently expel the boy from his class.

"What you did was wrong. You will receive a zero for the quiz," Mr. Marshall offered, "and we can start from square one. You will need to regain my confidence. You need to rebuild the trust between us."

I agreed with Mr. Marshall's decision, and then I added, "And I think, Ly, that you owe Mr. Marshall an apology."

The boy said how upset he felt as he once again wiped away tears. He said again that he had never cheated before, and then, as if choreographed by the gods, Ly Sing stood up, turned to Mr. Marshall, and bowed slowly. "I am sorry, Mr. Marshall." The gesture of this young boy bending his body in a slight, powerful gesture of apology, the quiet words, "I am sorry, Mr. Marshal," here I witnessed a true path to forgiveness.

As the boy turned to leave my office, I said, "Ly Sing, you are a very brave young man." He didn't turn in my direction but rather, walked out into the hallway and disappeared.

"Ly Sing will be just fine, Mr. Marshall," I said as the teacher returned to his classes, and I returned to my desk and began to sharpen some pencils.

Most of the time people do not want us to sign our names with a pencil. Checks, driver's licenses, legal documents all require a signature using a pen. I never sign a book with a pencil.

I am surprised that, despite all our fancy technology, our signature is still a powerful, legally accepted mark. When we sign our names to a document, we are saying, "Here I am, uniquely. No one else." The choices we make, acts of contrition, acts of forgiveness, the courage we display during times of deep regret, explain who we are.

Lord Have Mercy

The sun will be turned to darkness
and the moon to blood
before the coming of the great and
glorious day of the Lord.

Acts 2:20

I usually sleep late on Saturday morning because, like most of us, I am tired and that is the one time of the week when all schedules are off. I cannot recall the last time I abandoned my bed on a Saturday morning before eight-thirty.

Recently I decided to see what it would be like to set my Friday night alarm clock for the usual morning wake-up call of 6:00. I intended to dress and see what I would discover in the early hours of the new weekend.

At six that particular Saturday morning the alarm, as usual, didn't ring, for I always wake a few minutes before the clock screams. I whacked the button down before the harsh sound had a chance to do its job. I looked at the illuminated dial across from my sleeping wife and thought about the traffic jams, until I quickly remembered that there was no snake of a commute waiting to whip me up and down its twisting back but rather, a simple horse of an early morning walk waiting to carry me peacefully along the way to an uncertain destination.

I quickly showered, dressed, ate a bit of yogurt, and drank a glass of orange juice. The family slept. The dog slept. I quietly unlocked the side door and jumped over the four steps leading to the driveway. I was free. I was not seeking freedom, but that is the first thing I discovered along the way that morning, an inner sense of letting go for a moment. Another hard week was behind me. The hard week was ahead of me, but at that moment, all of

Saturday stood before me like wet mortar between the bricks: still loose and moist between the solid blocks of time that, eventually, will form the structure of my life.

At the end of the driveway I had to decide if I was going to turn right or turn left. To the right: town and the newspaper. To the left: a housing development. I heard the roar of the highway in the distance. A garbage truck coughed and spit down the next street. And then the rain.

I slowly walked up the four laughing steps back into the house, unzipped my coat, hung it on the coatrack, slipped off my shoes, walked into the living room and lay down flat on my back on the blue carpet. Silence.

So this is Saturday morning, I thought as I closed my eyes. I was about to sleep when I felt a sloppy tongue against my cheek, and then I saw a black nose and a shaggy face between two droopy, shaggy ears. If the dog could talk, it would have said, "Hi, Chris! Hi! Good morning! Hi! Wagging tail! See my tail? Oh, boy! What are you doing here so early? Want to play? Huh? Boy, oh, boy, this is great!"

I brushed the dog aside and rolled on my belly. It hopped on my back and started sniffing my neck, then pushed its head against my shoulder, rolled over sideways, draped itself upside down, hung out its tongue then sneezed. "Come on, Chris. Scratch me on my belly like you do sometimes!"

I scratched the dog on its belly. It rolled over, crouched, jumped, licked me on the face, crouched again. "Come on, take me for a walk!"

"It's raining," I said. Perhaps the phrase, *It's raining*, means "Yeah, let's go for a great walk," for the dog turned and, as in a cartoon, ran to the side door.

"Bark! Bark! Come on, Chris!" Jump. Shake floppy ears. Sneeze. "Let's go! Bark! Bark!"

I dipped my feet back into my shoes, reacquainted my rumpled coat to my rumpled body, hooked the leash to the dog's collar, and quietly opened the side door. The dog jumped over the four steps. I quickly followed, and we were off, running down the driveway, zooming right, heading for town. "Come on, Chris!" The dog pulled like a fish on a line.

By the time we arrived at the newspaper store, the rain stopped. I bought a biscuit for the dog, a bagel, and the newspaper. We sat on the small brick wall just to the left of the milk store. As the dog chewed its bone, I read an article about doctors helping to unearth victims of the massacres in Bosnia: flesh still intact revealing faces. Men, women, and children with gashes in their crushed skulls. There was a description of a mother with her child still strapped to her back, both with crushed skulls. The newspaper article explained that the physical evidence was needed to bolster eyewitness accounts. The combined information will be useful in the attempt to seek justice in a world court.

The dog's nose appeared under the paper. I scratched her head and gave her the rest of my bagel. I looked down the street to the left and then to the right. A single car passed. Its rubber tires, rolling against the pavement, offered the only audible sounds.

What is the sound of a bullet being imbedded in the skull of a child? Where were the child and mother going? How is it that the straps held them together in their death and in their grave? What horrible power allows the human hand to lift a gun to the head of a two-year-old boy?

As I stood up, the dog wagged its tail and was ready for our return trip home. As I walked past a trash barrel beside the Sweet Shop, I pitched the newspaper into the air. It fluttered, flapped, attempted to fly, flopped down on the rim of the round barrel, wobbled back and forth a bit, then fell into the dark mouth of the empty barrel. I heard the newspaper's thud.

By the time we reached the house, the dog was tired. She slowly climbed the four steps up to the door. I opened the door. Twelve-year-old Karen greeted me. "Where were you, Daddy?"

"The dog and I went for a walk."

"On Saturday?"

"Yeah. I just wanted to see what I could find so early in the morning."

"Did you find anything?" Karen asked as she was about to open the kitchen cabinet for her cereal.

"No," I said as I stroked her beautiful hair. "I just bought the dog a biscuit, and I read a bit of the newspaper." And then I kissed Karen's head, and I wanted to cry. We know that God gave man the power to choose between good or evil; we just can't believe we don't always choose good.

Sometimes there simply is no explanation to the evil that stains the mural of life. When I was a child, someone said to me that a sin creates a stain on our souls. I watched intently as my grandmother rubbed the jelly out of my shirt one afternoon. Perhaps, I figured, if I drank enough water and jumped up and down vigorously, my soul, like my shirt, would be cleansed of the blue stain, the blue-jelly stain of my evil ways, evil for not admitting I broke the living room window. I felt, at that time in my life, that evil could be beaten, could be adjusted. I had, in my power, the ability to change the darkness inside me. And I always felt better. I always felt a light of forgiveness.

Who is forgiven in the massacre of thousands and thousands of people? Who is forgiven? How do we combat such evil? The stones are thrown. Who stands between the life lived and the life taken away? Are we invisible to the spear of evil's death? Are we immune to such pain? Heat and moisture nurture the rose in spring. What is cold and dry strangles the movement of life.

Let us be the heat of faith. In his wisdom, God allows our faith to be the heat and moisture to a parched, lifeless world. I kiss my daughter so that she may live in peace and confidence and so that she may carry with her the message from the father: Love me and so I am loved, and so I am capable of giving love, and where I go so shall evil part from the road and fall to the side and perish in the dust.

Middle-Age

The moon marks off the seasons.

Psalm 104:19

The reality of middle age becomes painful when we stop dreaming, but if the dreams persist we are lulled through the pain toward acceptance and renewed vigor.

On the first Saturday morning of this month, as I have done for the past eighteen years, I intended to hang the Christmas wreath outside against the second-story window.

I tunneled my arms into my winter coat, stepped out into the cold air, grumbled my way through the alley between the house and the garage, and crawled under the deck where the aluminum ladder stretched out like the skeleton of a silver-boned giraffe. Same house. Same deck. Same ladder. Different man, different enough from the man who, twenty-four years ago, was a sophomore in college, reciting poems by Yeats, to women who draped themselves on yellow divans.

As I dragged the stubborn ladder from under the deck, I smacked my head on a low beam of wood. If I had been ten, I would have cried. If I had been twenty I would have sworn. I, a forty-four-year-old man, reached up, placed my hand on the back of my head and imagined it was the hand of someone else: a mother, a lover, a comfort warm and sweet, until the idea of hanging the Christmas wreath returned into my throbbing skull.

I waddled out from under the deck, pulled the ladder behind me back through the alley, past the car, and then I set it up against the front of the house.

As I stood at the foot of the ladder with the wreath looped around one of my arms, I looked up to the second-story window and sighed. *Some people leave their Christmas decorations up all year,* I thought as I began my ascent one step at a time.

My hands were cold. My head hurt. I was tired. No one was out in the neighborhood. I didn't want to hang the Christmas wreath. I thought about my size 34 waist. I thought about my bald spot. By the time I reached the top of the ladder, I was Willy Lowman, that lost man in Arthur Miller's play, *Death of a Salesman*. I, like Willy, wished someone would pay attention to me.

That is when I realized that the gutters were choked with fallen oak leaves, for I had forgotten to clean them the month before.

Because the ladder fell short of the roof, I was not able to look into the gutter. I just felt my way and grabbed the leaves.

JAB! JAB! A needle, or what felt like a needle, shot through my index finger. I had inadvertently grabbed a dormant bee curled inside the dry leaves. I reeled back with such pain and surprise that I forgot I was sixteen feet up in the air. I lost my balance. The wreath fell to the ground. I quickly grabbed the edge of the gutter, and swayed back and forth a few times until I regained my balance and my sure-footed position at the top of the ladder.

My hands were still cold. My head still hurt. I was still tired, and my finger was throbbing, but then I looked down at the green wreath with its red bow, and I realized how easily I could have been smashed against the brick stairs with stains of my own blood crisscrossed in ribbons against my ruined body. That is when I laughed aloud like the enlightened Scrooge.

I laughed, thinking about whacking my head under the deck. I laughed as I sucked the pain out of my finger. I shot down the ladder like a fireman, scooped up the wreath, climbed back up the ladder, and tied the evergreen to the nail I had hammered above the window eighteen years ago. "Beautiful nail. Rusted nail. Christmas nail."

I nearly rode the ladder back under the deck, patted the low-hanging beam with a jaunty slap, then I ran into the house and announced to Roe as I reached for the car keys, "I'm going to Shop-Rite!"

"But what for?" Roe asked with a smile, recognizing my light-hearted demeanor.

"Secret. Christmas, you know."

I bought Michael, our ten-year-old son, the five-foot toy bear I saw in the supermarket the week before for $39.95. When Roe and I first saw the bear, I thought it would be a Tiny-Tim-type gift for Michael, but then I dismissed the bear as frivolous, useless, and expensive.

Just after I nearly fell off the ladder, all my ghosts of Christmas past returned to me: the tin race car I found in my stocking one year; the cat that climbed the Christmas tree one Christmas eve and how my father was able to finally coax it down with a shake from the cat's box of food. I remembered the people singing Christmas songs in the nursing home across the street. I remembered the first Christmas that Roe and I spent together dreaming of children to come. I remembered the stockings tacked to the door. I remembered David, Karen, and Michael walking in single file down the stairs on Christmas morning.

Remember how, after *his* revelation, Scrooge flung open his bedroom window and called down to the boy on the street? Remember how he asked the boy if he knew about the large turkey in the butcher's window? "The one as big as me?" the boy called out.

Yes, indeed, that was the turkey the new Scrooge wished to send over to Bob Cratchit and his family.

This Christmas, Michael is receiving a frivolous, useless, five-foot brown bear, a gift from his father, his forty-four-year-old, balding father, Michael's ghost of Christmas Present with a bump on his head and a bee sting in his finger, this man who still dreams about yellow divans and tin racing cars, and who, as old Scrooge said " . . . will honor Christmas in my heart, and try to keep it all the year."

The Search for Christmas

Magi from the east came to Jerusalem and asked
"Where is the one who has been born king of the Jews?"

Matthew 2:1 – 2

Each year I write a Christmas story. During the year I wrote my novel, *The Summer Soldier*, I spent much time thinking about Jackie and his sister, Sarah, the little boy and girl I created.

I based the characters on a number of influences: the children in the novel *To Kill a Mockingbird*, my sister, Anne, and me when we were young, and on my own daughter, Karen.

The things to listen for the most in the story are the voices of the boy and girl. They carry in their hearts a deep sense of grief, but such sadness enriched their attitudes about life. We can all learn from these children during their search for Christmas.

Now I'm not supposed to tell you about the day Christmas crashed down the front hall stairs, because I promised Sarah I wouldn't tell, but as I always figured, what's the use of knowing something without telling about it?

I don't blame Sarah right out, but I blame that she was clumsy. I heard that when she was born the doctor praised her long fingers and toes. They say that people born with long fingers and toes become great artists. Those people obviously didn't include my sister, Sarah, in their research for she was just clumsy. She never became an artist.

We made a bet, my sister and I, back then when it was worth taking risks. I remember one afternoon when I was eleven, Sarah, who was eight, pretended that she was fifty-three.

"Sarah?" I asked real meanly, "Why'd you pick such a dumb number like fifty-three to pretend?" She'd looked at me like I was a worm and puffed out her cheeks. "Dorothy Canfield's mother is fifty-three and Dorothy has a silk pocketbook." I couldn't figure out what a silk pocketbook had to do with pretending you were fifty-three. And Mrs. Canfield was forty-two. I knew that because she was the same age my mother would have been back in 1963, the year I'm telling you about.

"I bet I can find Christmas before you can," Sarah said in early December as she and I sat on the stoop, chipping away at the ice with yellow-handled screwdrivers.

"What do you mean *find Christmas*?" I asked as I stabbed the ice again and again.

"Well, I know where my bicycle is." Sarah dropped her screwdriver and began clearing the snow away from the ice.

"What's that got to do with Christmas, you old goat?"

Sarah didn't like being called a goat. She liked being called old not only because she liked pretending that she was fifty-three, but she also liked pretending that she was an airline pilot. She saw once in a magazine a woman airline pilot. This woman, she had a captain's hat on and brass buttons on her coat. She looked old, according to Sarah.

But I learned never to call Sarah a goat unless I meant it and unless I was willing to get bitten. I could tease and tease Sarah, but if I didn't mean it she'd just sit there and think, usually about a way to get even like the time she dumped her chocolate ice-cream cone between my sheets. I thought I squashed our new kitten when I pushed my feet down there. The ice-cream was all melted by the time I went to bed, and the cone was soggy. It felt like a kitten's head but smeared all over the inside on my sheets.

But if I said something like calling her a goat and I meant it, Sarah would believe that her feet were turning into hooves and that her chin was growing a beard and she'd just jump up at me as quick as she could and bite. Sarah believed that the faster you made something go away, the better the chances were that it didn't exist in the first place. Whenever she bit me on the leg, you could see her teeth marks for a week.

"My bicycle's in the garage," Sarah said as she looked at herself in the smooth ice she polished with her green mittens.

"What's that got to do with Christmas?" I asked. I gave up trying to clear the ice from the stoop. I stood up in my buckled, black boots and began sliding back and forth between the iron railings.

"Well," Sarah said as she leaned closer and closer to her distorted image in the ice, "do you think I look like an airline pilot?"

I was about to say that she looked like a goat, but then I remembered Dracula, so I just ignored her question. I was about to ask her the Christmas question again when she stood up and looked at me eye to eye. Well, not eye to eye exactly. I slipped on the ice and fell next to her. She crossed her eyes funny-like, then said, "Well, I haven't seen my bike in a week, but I know it's in the garage."

"So?" I said. I tried to stand up again on the ice, but Sarah sat down next to me and held my hand. She had never held my hand before except for the day they had the funeral for my mother and father. Well, they were Sarah's mother and father, too, but I never looked at them that way, belonging to both Sarah and me at the same time. I thought once that parents had the ability to belong to each son and daughter the same way a cat belongs to no one in particular in the family, but each person believes it belongs to him.

The night I thought I killed the kitten with my feet, I felt awful. I kept thinking, *My cat! My cat!* When I reached down and pulled out Sarah's soggy ice-cream cone, I was going to burn Sarah's room down. Brothers never feel as if they own a sister. I drew a picture of a goat and tacked it on her door.

My mother and father were writers. They drove out to Spring Lake, that's by the ocean. They had a party about a friend's book. On the way home there was an accident. I don't know if the truck jumped in front of their car, or if their car jumped in front of the truck, but I know that from that night on I never believed in what I couldn't see ever again. Not Sarah, though.

"I know my bike's in the garage. Don't you get it?" She squeezed my hand. I shook away from her grip, but she held on, keeping my blue glove.

"Gimme my glove," I said.

"You can know something without seeing it," Sarah continued. "And if you know something, it's got to be somewhere." Sarah took my glove and continued to polish her patch of ice. "So I bet Christmas is somewhere. I saw it last year. I don't see it now, so it must be somewhere."

I looked at Sarah as she knelt on the front step and smoothed over the dull ice.

The accident happened in September that year and our grandparents came to live with us in the house. They thought it was best that things didn't change much more in our lives, so they sold their Chicago house and moved here with us in New Jersey. Trouble was we were in the second week of December and there was no tree, the cards weren't taped around the living room windows, and the yellow plastic bells my mother took care of each year weren't hanging from the handles on the kitchen cabinet.

"Once you know a thing, there's got to be a place for it," Sarah said as she threw my glove into the evergreen bush beyond the right railing.

"Hey, get my glove!" I was going to push her, but then she called me a chicken. Sarah had the ability to make you stop doing things because she got you thinking about something else.

"Chicken about what?" I asked.

"Look in the ice, Jackie." She pointed with her right hand balled up in her mitten.

I leaned over with my sister, and the two of us looked into the dull ice. All I saw was a vague image of a little girl and a little boy looking back at us.

"See?" Sarah whispered. "Here we are, but we don't know it unless we look in a mirror. We also got a place."

I thought that maybe Sarah's long toes were curling into her shoes, which caused the blood to clot down there and smear her brain like the ice-cream cone did to my sheets, but then she called me a chicken again, saying I was afraid to make a bet with her, and then she pushed me over the stoop and I fell backward into the snow.

"I bet you a dollar I can find Christmas first. It's gotta be somewhere, like my bike. Do you wanna bet or don't you?" She stood up and leaned against the iron railing. I stood up, walked over to the evergreen, leaned over, picked up my glove and, like I'd seen in a Robin Hood movie, I threw my glove at Sarah's feet and said "I bet you *two* dollars I'll find it first."

Sarah stomped on my glove, spun around on the ice, opened the front door, walked into the house, stuck her tongue out at me, and yelled, "You're on," then she slammed the door and locked it.

I picked up the two screwdrivers, ground my shoe against the smooth part of the ice Sarah had made, then I rang the doorbell.

"Jackie Carton, I see you standing there," my grandmother said as she opened the door. "What I can't see is why you'd ring the doorbell to your own house."

"Sarah locked me out. And she threw my glove in the snow," I said as I entered the house. I pulled my other glove off my hand, peeled my coat from my shoulders, and then I smelled ginger.

"Where's Sarah?" I asked, hoping she wasn't eating all the gingerbread cookies my grandmother was obviously making in the kitchen.

"She's in the basement, rummaging around looking for something. She took a flashlight. Don't you two start up, and be here in twenty minutes to taste my cookies. They're cooling."

I ran down the basement stairs, flicked on the light, and found Sarah in the far corner opposite the furnace under a pile of clothes.

"That's not fair," I said. "You got a head start."

"Christmas isn't hidden here," Sarah said as she stood up with a woman's fancy green hat on her head. She was standing in the pile of Good Will clothes, things to be given to the poor.

"Jackie, did you ever wonder why these clothes smell so nice?"

Many of the clean dresses and blue suits were new. Some even had the tags on them. I didn't tell Sarah that these clothes belonged to our parents. I never told her that.

"Sarah, what part of Christmas do you think you are looking for?"

She looked at me, the same way she looked at me when I called her a goat. She knew I meant what I said. I didn't know what she was looking for. Half the trick is to know what you are looking for.

"Christmas, Jackie. I'm looking for like-always Christmas."

We looked behind the furnace, under the dusty workbench, inside the game closet, to the left and right of the washing machine. No Christmas.

"Maybe in the attic?" Sarah asked.

We lumbered up the basement stairs. Sarah shook the flashlight and we both watched the dull point of light zigzag back and forth on the walls. Sarah turned around, pointed the flashlight under her chin, and growled.

As we walked into the living room at the top of the stairs, we both smelled the fresh cookies. I was about to turn in the direction of the kitchen when Sarah reminded me of our bet. She ran ahead, turned left, and disappeared up the stairs to the second floor. By the time I reached the hall, Sarah was already clomping up the stairs to the attic.

Children believe in what they can see. Very young children believe that when something disappears from their view, it no longer exists. The older we become the more we understand the physical properties of motion and stillness. We accept that an empty glass has the ability to hold a certain amount of water. We have the need to store things for the future; we create places; we understand "here" and "gone." Some people, mostly those people who read, or those who have long fingers and toes, believe that if you search long enough you'll find what you are looking for.

By the time I reached the top step to the attic, Sarah was already walking toward the stairs with five brightly painted tin boxes stacked in her arms.

"I think you owe me two dollars," Sarah said smugly. I tried to argue with her in an attempt to protect my money, but she brushed past me and began to walk quickly down the stairs.

"Sarah! Wait a minute!" I turned and began to follow her. By the time she reached the second floor, she was running. I began to chase after her. "Sarah! Wait!" She turned to her left, trying as best she could to balance the boxes in her arms as she began to jump down the hall stairs. I was about to call her an old goat, when she tripped and fell down the last five steps. As I said, Sarah was clumsy. The tin boxes crashed and exploded on the wood floor. Christmas bulbs popped. Tin soldiers slid into the radiator. The box with the crèche rolled against the wall and split open. The donkey's head broke off. Mary and Joseph landed under the bed of straw. Sarah was on her stomach. Her arms were sprawled out before her. Glass stars, Christmas ornaments, the dancing Santa Claus music box, Christmas lights, all were spread out the downstairs hall like the leftover ruins of a tornado. My grandmother and I reached Sarah at the same time. As we stood over her, I wanted to call her a clumsy oaf, but before I could savor the new triumph, especially after losing two dollars, my grandmother held her right index finger against her tightly closed lips and squeezed my left shoulder. I closed my mouth and looked down at Sarah.

"Are you all right?" my grandmother asked.

Sarah didn't speak. She nodded, picked herself up a bit, and then stayed in a kneeling position. She looked up at my grandmother, then she looked up at me. She was at the "I'm-about-to-cry" stage, when she looked down at the scattered Christmas trinkets and suddenly spoke out, "Here it is! I found it!" Sarah reached over for a small, green cloth bag. "I found it, Jackie!"

Sarah stood up and ran into the kitchen carrying the bag in both hands. I looked at my grandmother and shrugged as we both followed my sister into the kitchen.

Sarah, trying to hide her tears, was already hanging up a third yellow, plastic bell on a kitchen cabinet, and we didn't interrupt her as she finished attaching all the yellow bells on each door handle, the same bells our mother had hung each Christmas as far back as we could remember.

When Sarah finished, she stood back and said, "I knew I'd find it."

That afternoon, after we cleaned the hallway, taped up the Christmas cards, and bought a tree, Sarah, my grandmother, and I ate all the gingerbread cookies.

Without my seeing, it snowed that night, and well into the next morning.

Waning

Moon

Hidden Places of the Heart

Youth gets together his materials to build a bridge to the moon.

Henry David Thoreau
Journal, January 2, 1852

In *To Kill a Mockingbird*, the neighborhood recluse, Boo Radley, hid small gifts for the children, Scout and Jem, inside a rotten knot hole in the trunk of an old tree. As the children walked past, they would periodically find gum, marbles, little statues, and other small trinkets. These were gifts offered by the shy, slow, simple and good Boo, who protected the children and eventually saved their lives.

We human beings like to hide things in tight places. I remember how pleased I was as a child when I discovered inside my new pair of jeans a small pocket hidden inside my larger pocket. After my father explained that such was the place to keep coins, I immediately found a nickel and stuffed it deep inside the magic pouch.

I remember a high school friend who invited me to his home for dinner. He revealed a secret slot he had created in his wood-paneled bedroom. With the pull of a hidden string, part of a panel slid open and exposed a small chamber the size of a shoe box. Inside the wall my friend kept his money, a genuine Joe DiMaggio autograph, and a picture of Laura Tarpy, the prettiest girl in our freshman class.

I have my own hiding place.

Soon after my wife, Roe, and I became parents for the first time, we were walking with our new son, David, through a church craft fair. We looked at the fancy candles, the quilts, and the sweet jams. At one table a woman was selling toys. David was just an infant, but we thought that he might like the small green plastic turtle, the yellow bumblebee, and the brown owl with wide eyes.

These were finger puppets, but Roe suggested that they would make good bathtub toys.

Roe was right. The small figures made for terrific bathtub toys, so much so that we began a collection: Mickey Mouse, a brown bear, Ernie and Bert from "Sesame Street."

Over the years, reaching in for the basket of little toys under the sink became a routine for all of our three children, David, Karen, and Michael, when they bathed in the tub. They liked to line up the creatures along the edge of the tub or on the top of the hot and cold faucets. They played with the bee and turtle, with Mickey and Bert, until the bath water lost its heat and its entertainment.

Late one evening, when Roe and the children were asleep for the night, I reached down for the filled garbage can in the kitchen, and was about to carry the pail outside when I noticed, wedged under a squashed milk carton, a small shade of green. I picked the carton up from the pile of trash and there, in a jumble of disorder and finality, rested Mickey, Bert and Ernie, the owl, the bee, and the small, green turtle. Roe, recognizing that the children had outgrown the finger puppets, threw out the faded, soap-filled, useless toys.

Like a claw in one of those arcade machines, my hand reached down into the trash bin and rescued each figure one by one. After I rinsed each creature in the kitchen sink, I placed it on the kitchen table until the collection was complete. If the plastic owl could have talked it would have said, "Take us back to the bathroom. Where are the children who used the sponge as a raft to sail the bee across the fierce waves to save the turtle who was being attacked by the soap? We haven't gone out to sea in over a year!"

I gathered up the little creatures into my cupped hands and was about to toss them back into the garbage, but then I slipped the owl onto one of my fingers, wiggled it a bit, placed the rest on my other fingers and walked into the living room. I was going to keep these plastic toys, my treasures, the little beings that fit between the fingers of my babies.

Knowing that Roe would be teasingly annoyed with my sentimentality, I decided to hide the finger puppets. Where? Where? I descended the stairs of the basement like a pirate about to bury his loot. I looked behind the furnace, inside a closet, and under the stairs until, finally, I noticed the hole in the ceiling.

The summer before, Roe and I hired a company to install a new oil furnace that needed new pipes. The old pipes and furnace were removed, and the new heating unit was set in place. Because the new heating system didn't match the old system, a hole was left in the basement ceiling. That is where I hid the children's old toys. One by one, I carefully placed each character inside the ceiling. I had to push them deeply inside so that they could not be seen accidentally. Then I went to bed.

Bert and Ernie, Mickey, turtle, bee, and owl still sit in the darkness of the basement ceiling.

Why do I keep things hidden in little places? Because someday Roe and I will have grandchildren splashing in the tub. The waves will rise. The soap shark will once again seek vengeance, and the sponge raft will again carry turtle and the rest to the safety of an old man's open hands, a man who remembered other days, other seas, other waves crashing against his laughing heart.

Lost at Sea

Lady Moon, Lady Moon, whom are you loving?

Baron Houghton (1809–1885)

I received a phone call today from Fred, one of my closest friends. He wanted to share with me his loss of a high school friend he had known for fifty-five years. "Chris, I have known him longer than you have been alive. I feel there is an empty space inside me. I wanted to call and share this with you."

I wanted to tell Fred that I understood, and the best way I could explain such understanding was to share with him a loss I had experienced.

A few days before my grandmother died, I was able to speak with her on the telephone. She was dying in a hospital in Brussels, Belgium. "Oh, Christopher," she said. "Oh, Christopher." She wasn't weeping. She wasn't in pain. As she simply repeated my name, all the memories of my grandmother flew out through the international telephone cable: her singing French songs about my grandfather riding a horse, her laughter when my sister Anne and I performed a circus in the attic with our cat, Tiger Lily. My grandmother: her perfume, her worn slippers, her housedress and brown stockings. She liked butterscotch and port and ice cream and card games, and she loved me.

I began to tell Fred that I understood that empty feeling as I spoke about my grandmother, but then I realized that my grandmother's dying didn't say all that I wanted to say about loss. After all, she was ninety-two when she died. Her death was expected. When my grandfather died, I didn't feel that pang of loss, for I was too young, and he always frightened me with his gruff ways. My parents are still alive, and, well, I was holding back, not saying how much I understood about Fred's empty feeling, but then I found myself speaking about love.

When I love someone deeply, it is unconditional. It is difficult to share this unconditional love with everyone, for it would exhaust me. We are built to love one another, that I am sure of, but I also believe we are built to love one another in different ways. We love the stranger as a fellow pilgrim. We recognize universal traits in this person: the history of our mutual existence, the charity and labor of our distinctly different yet similar lives.

Then we have acquaintances, people we know in our neighborhood, in our schools, and in our daily work. We exchange words, jokes, mutual concerns about superficial things. There is a respect and affection much of the time. But I wanted to share with Fred the loss of someone who was a deep part of me.

I have always known that to reveal the hidden layers of myself places me at risk: the risk of being laughed at, the risk of being misunderstood, the risk of harming those that I love, but then I have also learned that it is our essential nature to divulge what is closest to our hearts with others. It is like sharing secrets. We like to share secrets.

I want to tell you about Betty. We human beings *fall in love*. I like that phrase because it has a sound and sense that defines an image and a way of being: We do fall, dive, tumble out of ourselves, down into the other when we are in love. And what is love? A time divided equally between two people who choose to labor and sing in unison.

For two years I sang and labored with Betty, though I eventually realized that most of the singing and labor came from my own heart, for such was the imbalance of our time together that led her to leave me.

I met this young woman in college. She was the first woman I loved. She was not the first woman I dated, for there were many young women, but I always felt there was something missing along the way. We cannot teach young people the ingredients of love. It is different for each person, yet the same for us all.

I loved Betty. She liked to sing in the car. She spent her summers working at a camp for handicapped children. She made silver jewelry. She loved children's books, the theater, the ocean. Betty was, in my eyes, a beautiful woman. She loved her mother and father and her sister, Barbara, and her brother, Rick. I loved her voice, her laugh, her handwriting, her letters.

Betty and I walked one afternoon to the top of the Palisade cliffs in New Jersey. There was a path that Betty knew. We had to climb rocks, descend into small gullies, and then climb some more. At one point, as she was struggling a few feet above me, I found a wildflower. I picked the flower, and when the two of us reached the top of the cliff, I said, "Betty?"

"Yes," she answered.

"Close your eyes."

She faced me and closed her eyes. Of course, now I realize that she had expected me to kiss her; instead, I held the flower out before me and then I said, "Now open."

She opened her eyes, looked at me, and then at the flower. She pulled the flower from my hand and hooked it into her hair.

When I finally asked her to marry me a few months later, she had few words. "I'm not good enough for you." What she was really saying, I think, was that she did not *fall in love* with me, she did not fall, dive, tumble out of herself and into my heart.

Today Betty is, perhaps, more myth than reality. I haven't seen her in over twenty years, but it is one of my great hopes . . . to someday see her again.

My good wife, the woman who fell in love with me at the same time I fell in love with her, knows about Betty, as any wife would know about her husband's former wife who had died. Roe knows I loved Betty. There is plenty of room to love many women in my heart, but to love Roe and Betty the way I love these women cannot be filled by more than one person at a time, for in such love, such unconditional love, there is that equal time, that mutual song and labor that is shared.

There were moments when I felt that Betty and I were approaching that time, and there are years and years, and photographs, and children, and nights, and vacations, and defeats and victories, and Christmases and thunderstorms, and winters and candy corn that Roe and I have shared together in all the wide and holy years we have been together in our marriage. But there was a brief time when I also was in love with another woman, and when she decided that she wasn't in love with me, I experienced a loss, an emptiness that has never left me. We risk such loss when we deeply love someone else. We risk losing a part of ourselves: water down the stream, down the stream, down the stream. Water down the stream spreading out wide down to the sea.

Betty is lost to that sea of my past, and she took with her a young man in his twenties who picked wildflowers and who regrets not having kissed her.

That is the loss I shared with Fred as he spoke about the loss of his good friend. "Yes," he agreed, "that is what I also feel."

When I least expect it, I discover the moon poking through the trees. I suppose I could read in the newspaper about the next cycle of the moon, but then I wouldn't be surprised. We need surprises in our lives.

Sometimes when I am out shopping, or walking through the streets of New York City on a visit, I see a woman who, in a small surprise, reminds me of Betty: the hair, a certain laugh, a tone of voice, an image poking through the trees of my memory, those long branches reaching back into my early roots of discovery. We cannot forget those roots, or deny their existence. We need, to maintain a balanced life, to bathe ourselves in the moonlight of our past, for it is there that we felt the first warmth of a certain light that defines who we really are, and such warmth deflects the night's cold when we feel tired or lonely or just old and nearly forgotten.

Roe and our three children sustain the person I have become. My grandmother, Betty, and wildflowers sustain the person that I was, and in the end they are both who I am, past and present, and so the balance is maintained, and the lady moon disappears behind the clouds, and I can sleep.

Let Me Go Adventuring

I walk unseen
On the dry smooth-shaven green,
To behold the wandering moon,
Riding near her highest noon,
Like one that had been led astray
Through the heav'n's wide pathless way,
And oft, as if her head she bowed,
Stooping through a fleecy cloud.

John Milton (1608 – 1674)

Perhaps it is true. Perhaps we Americans have lost the need for real adventure. A soft padded chair in a movie theater is better than a saddle. A computer keyboard is more exciting than a mountain trail. Did we lose the spirit to wander when we, as a people, reached the Pacific Ocean? Have we lost the courage to follow the moon as it leads us through the darkness?

It seems that we are more and more satisfying our sense of wonder and curiosity with vicarious experiences by way of the television camera in space shuttles, in court rooms, and on football fields.

Perhaps this is why I bought a 1929 Model A Ford.

While on vacation this past summer, my wife's hair dryer flashed, popped, and then zapped the carpet with a small burn. She tossed the machine into the trash. Ten minutes later, Peter, my brother-in-law, retrieved the broken appliance, unscrewed the casing, fiddled with the wires, secured the casing once again, and plugged in the contraption. A steady, even flow of warm air wafted in my direction.

Peter was the first person I called to say, "I bought something." He was astonished that I, who can't tell the difference between a carburetor and a soda can, I who would buy a new hair dryer rather than attempt to surgically remove the defect of the old machine with a screwdriver ... how could *I* possibly be interested in a 1929 Model A Ford?

My wife believes I am entering a midlife crisis. My children think that I just wanted a big toy. A fellow who heard about my recent purchase pulled into my driveway in *his* 1930 Model A and invited me to join the antique automobile club.

During our conversation, when I told him I do not know anything about engines, he asked me, "Well, why'd you get the car, then?" He drove off without the usual *Ahooogah* farewell.

At first I didn't even understand why I had purchased the car from my friend who had retired from banking after forty years. "It just sat in my basement," Jerry said as he handed me the bill of sale. "I drove it fifty miles in the last eight years."

Then I began thinking about John Glenn wedged inside a space capsule. I thought about Willa Cather's Antonia as she traveled across the rugged land in a covered wagon. I thought about my brother sleeping in the tree fort he built in the middle of the woods back when kids built tree forts. I thought about Charles Lindbergh and how he must have felt as *The Spirit of St. Louis* vibrated all around him. Then I began to understand what the "A" meant to me.

Imagine sitting in a car that smells like dust and wood and upholstery and oil. Imagine sitting in this car in the semidarkness of your garage. Imagine inserting a small key in a keyhole not to engage the ignition but to turn on the electric current. Imagine reaching over to the left side of the steering column and pushing the spark lever to the up position. Imagine moving the gas throttle down a single notch. Imagine pushing in the clutch, pulling out the choke, pressing the starter button. Imagine hearing a sudden groan and whine, then the classic bubble and purring sound ticking and popping under the hood.

I suspect there is a parallel feeling when people start a jet engine, light the burner of a hot air balloon, or release the sails: the beginning of an adventure. But there is something more.

While driving in the antique car, I feel as if I am wrapped in a blanket during a cold night, or, perhaps, encased in the womb. I feel transported to another time, a new place, a dream of rebirth. My little town seems different through the windshield of a Model A Ford.

Remember Toad's excitement in the book *The Wind in the Willows* as he drove about in his roadster?

> "Glorious, stirring sight!" murmured Toad ... "The poetry of motion! The real way to travel! The only way to travel! Here today—in next week tomorrow! Villages skipped, towns, cities jumped—always somebody else's horizons! O bliss! O poop-poop! O my! O my!"

The other day, as I drove my 1929 Ford along a back road, I came upon an old man leaning against a stone wall. As I zoomed by at thirty-two miles an hour, the man smiled and waved his cane above his head.

Ahooogah! Ahooogah! I pressed the silver button on the steering wheel.

The yellow spokes of my automobile turned and turned. The engine murmured, backfired, murmured some more. I, too, will someday lean against stone walls with my toothless grin. For now, let me go adventuring.

Ahooogah!

Sometimes, when I am tired, or alone I dare to push myself beyond my limitations. I answer one more letter, write one more essay, write one more poem. Often it is in this state of physical exertion that I slip into an unexpected surprise: a newly discovered way of making a connection between what I feel and what I see; a new idea for the next book; a renewed purpose for continuing a life that does not seem to rest.

Other times I am bored, or I give in to the fatigue, and then I sleep or complain. How to maintain a balance between doing and not doing is my daily challenge. If I know the rewards are great, a day's pay, a letter received, a kiss from a daughter, then it is easy to lift my head from my pillow and drag myself to the shower in the morning. If the rewards are hidden, I can easily lose faith.

What is in the human laughter that keeps us on the side of faith? I have always believed that if I keep at the labor, stick to the heartfelt responsibilities to those whom I love, if I maintain a daily argument with the mercurial world, then I know that I am alive, a participant, a fellow traveler on the way.

If I do not have my ticket in my hand, if I do not feel as if I am moving forward, if the stars stand still in the night's sky, then I know that there is no point in trying to create beauty. I'd probably think that all there is to living is watching television, waxing my car, consulting with my stockbroker, and drinking my soda.

Who is the new Adam among us? From where does he come? From what garden? Into what world?

The Burden and the Glory

Nothing that is can pause or stay;
The moon will wax, the moon will wane.

Henry Wadsworth Longfellow (1807–1882)

We spend our lives standing before a conveyor belt of experiences. People, days, chocolate, whispers, summer, books, events small and cataclysmic all pass before us. Such experiences become, in one way or another, a part of who we are.

In the late afternoon a few days ago, ten-year-old Michael opened the back door and exploded into the house with an announcement. His cheeks were blushed with November cold, his hands wrapped in mittens, his voice raced up and down a vocal scale that would have pleased any circus ringmaster.

"An owl! I saw an owl! It was this big!" And Michael extended his arms from one end of his imagination to the other. I looked at my son with a bit of doubt.

"Michael, an owl? On our street? Did you see it up close?"

"Dad, the guys and I were playing football, and this bird flew over us and landed in the pine tree just on top of our heads. I could see it real close. It had those ears that looked like horns, and he moved his head all around. He pooped twice."

Michael always loved the owl from the first moment I read to him "The Owl and the Pussycat went to sea," from the time I read to him the Arnold Lobel owl books; from the time Michael saw the owl in the zoo as it sat high on its perch and blinked.

Because Michael saw the owl pass before him on the conveyor belt of life, he was well-prepared for the owl's late afternoon visit on Woodland Court. Something appeared that triggered a response in Michael's mind. If Michael didn't know anything about owls, if he hadn't built an appreciation for this creature, he might not have been interested in the bird as it flew over the boys, casting a wide shadow over the lawn, or Michael might have, as someone suggested, wanted to kill the bird.

We human beings learn by building upon what we already know, and if we do not know something, it is the teacher's role, or the parent's role, or the book's role, or God's role to place that first bit of knowledge into a person's mind and heart. We human beings do stand before life's conveyor and absorb what passes before us on our own, but an experience is more powerfully imbedded in the mind if the experience is brought to the person with attention.

Roe and I are taking the children to Washington, D.C., to show them the extraordinary collection of the Vermeer paintings, the largest collection of the artist's works assembled since the 1600s. For the rest of their lives, our children will pay particular attention each time they hear Vermeer's name, or see one of his paintings.

The mind collects information, bounces such information back and forth against old knowledge, and then the mind creates new thoughts.

When I returned from work one afternoon, I was startled to see a pair of crutches on the kitchen table. Three years earlier, Karen had endured a terrible ordeal when doctors discovered a tumor in her foot that they clearly thought was cancer. My daughter was taken to the Sloane-Kettering Cancer Center in New York, where she had to have an operation to determine the condition of the tumor. Fortunately, the tumor was benign. For a number of weeks Karen supported herself with crutches. As the months, and then the years progressed, the tumor dissolved and Karen continued on her normal, happy life.

Crutches ... on the kitchen table. A rush of memories jumped to the surface. Karen's pain. The doctor's fears. The operation. The recovery room. Crutches. Crutches. Why are there crutches on the kitchen table? I walked into the living room and found Karen peacefully watching television.

"Hi, Daddy."

"Hi, Karen."

I wanted to weep all over again for my daughter's health and safety. I felt a sudden pang of a nearly forgotten stab in my heart.

"How are you, Karen?"

She looked at me in an odd way. "Okay."

"How was your day in school?" I asked as I looked at her legs she had propped up on the coffee table.

"Okay. I got an *A* on my science test."

Sloane-Kettering. Nurses. X-rays. Cancer. Doctors. Pain.

"Ah, Karen, does your foot hurt?"

"Huh?" Karen asked.

"Your leg? I saw the crutches."

Karen laughed. "Dad. I borrowed those crutches from the school nurse. I'm playing a part in a class play. I'm an injured football player." Then Karen turned her head a bit and quietly asked, "Dad, are you okay?"

"Yes, my girl." I turned, and as I walked into the kitchen, I gently stroked a single crutch and said aloud, "That's a terrific grade on your science test, Karen. Mom will be proud of you."

The crutch appeared on the conveyor belt, and my memories of Karen's suffering jumped back into the center of my life for a moment. See how our minds work?

Drew, a colleague at work, told me a story that explains the power of the mind. He and his wife, Barbara, buy a yearly subscription to the state theater. For a reasonable amount of money they attend six significant plays: Broadway hits, and some soon-to-be Broadway hits. I am interested in the theater, so I listened carefully to what Drew was saying in the office; however, the more he spoke, the more I realized that he was not telling me about the most recent play that he and his wife attended. He was telling me about this old man who sat next to him.

"There was this old, old man. The theater was warm. This was last week, the first week of November. Even though the theater was comfortably heated, this man, he was wearing gloves. He turned to me and said, 'I have weak circulation. My hands are always cold.'"

I couldn't understand why Drew was telling me about this man's gloves. Drew looked at me as if to say, "Don't you get it? Those gloves!"

I looked at Drew in such a way that obviously made him realize I had no idea what he was talking about, but then he quietly and powerfully and simply explained.

"When my father was dying, he had such poor circulation. He always complained about his cold hands, so he walked around the house with gloves on. No matter how warm the house was, his hands, they were cold, so he wore those gloves. The gloves. See?"

Drew's father died. He loved his father. Father, mentor, provider, counselor, friend. Cold, cold hands. Gloves, those gloves. When Drew saw the old man sitting next to him in the theater, wearing gloves to comfort his cold hands, Drew said he almost couldn't contain himself.

"The play wasn't much, but those gloves on that man's hands, they cut right into me."

Gloves pass before us on the conveyor belt. The owl, the crutches. Item after item, experience after experience, day by day we remember events, we store information into our hearts and minds. Poof! An owl flies over our heads and we shout with glee. Poof! A daughter was in pain once and we remember. Poof! The mind revolves, retains, rearranges new information to fit inside what is already learned, or felt.

The more experiences that pass before us, and the more we see, read, and feel, the more reflective we become, the smarter we are, the more pain and joy we will endure, but that is the burden and glory of what it means to be a human being.

In the Middle of the Woods

Viewed from the distance of the moon,
the astonishing thing about the earth
is that it is alive.

Lewis Thomas

My grandfather once told me that if I sit in the middle of the woods for a long enough time, whatever is hiding will eventually appear. In various ways I have always believed in this notion: When I was in seventh grade waiting for someone to pick me up at school following a snow storm, when I was a lonely young man hoping to someday meet my wife, when I was an expectant father, when I waited for the postman with news about my latest submitted manuscript. My father picked me up during the storm, my wife finally appeared in my life, my son was born, manuscripts were accepted. All these things were concealed, but I stuck around in the single place of my hopeful heart and eventually the revelations came to pass.

Because I was finally curious enough to test my grandfather's theory, I recently devoted a long Saturday afternoon to determine the veracity of his statement. I didn't tell Roe and the children. I imagined their reaction: "Dad, you're going to do what? Sit in the middle of the woods?"

I drove to my parents' house, parked the car, spent a few minutes with my mother and father, then I casually said that I was going for a long walk. I secretly stashed an apple in my pocket for a small bit of nourishment during the execution of my experiment.

"Be home around five for dinner," my mother suggested. I clearly understand my good fortune at my age to still have my mother and father, to still eat a meal my mother has prepared.

After I closed the door and walked through the garden for a few moments, I turned to look back at my parents' house, the house where I grew up, the house where my grandparents came to visit from Belgium each summer. The house that was once filled with six children, three cats, a hamster, a parakeet, and a family of squirrels.

I suspect that my grandfather's theory also works in reverse: Stick around long enough and things will disappear. My older brother lives in the next town. My one sister lives ninety miles west of the house; my other sister lives ninety miles south. My younger brother lives two hundred miles north. I live fifteen miles west. My second oldest brother died in 1980. The cats are gone, along with the hamster and parrot. My mother tells me with a smile, "At least the squirrels are still in the walls." But much is gone from the house.

As I entered the woods, I heard a rustling sound in the distance. Birds stopped singing. Crickets stopped rubbing their wings together. I walked to a large rock that sat like a tired elephant in the middle of the woods. I removed the apple from my pocket and placed it on the rock, and then I sat down and waited.

For some reason it is in my nature to wait patiently. As a child I liked to wait for my sister as she laced her skates down by the frozen pond that stretched out before us. I liked to wait for my father coming home from work, hoping to hear his familiar toot on the car's horn as he rumbled along the stone-covered driveway. I liked to sit on the kitchen stool and watch my mother make bread from start to finish. I especially liked watching her knead the dough.

So I, a forty-four-year-old man, sat on my rock in the middle of the woods. The first hour was easy, since I didn't expect anything to appear so soon, and it didn't. I looked deep within the trees above me hoping to spot a bird. No bird. I stared to my left, hoping to spot a rabbit. No rabbit.

The second hour was boring. I wondered if my grandfather's insight was based on his old age for, I suppose, if we reach a certain age most hidden things will eventually be revealed to us.

Nothing was revealed to me in the second hour of my vigil in the woods.

At the start of the third hour I was hungry, so I reached down for my apple, which was covered with ants. Ants! I waited two hours for stirring creatures of the woods to reveal themselves to me and all I saw were ants! And yet we cannot guess at the significance of a revelation. We sometimes expect a thunderstorm when, instead, the wind blows. We sometimes hope for a peaceful heart, and we get a day filled with loud children. We sometimes pray for the end of an illness for a loved one, but instead there is death; however, in the wind, deep inside the loud voices of the children, in a sudden death there appears hidden truths we did not know existed until the fruits of our patience were harvested, tasted, and eaten.

Ants. I followed the line of ants that extended from the apple, down the left side of the rock and into the earth. I would never have known that there was an ant nest deep inside the earth beside the elephant rock. Significant ants, hidden creature of the woods, companions ... messengers from my grandfather.

After I admired the ants for a few moments, I stood up, left the apple behind, and then I stepped off the rock. I walked backward for a few moments, watched the rock and the apple shrink in the distance, and then *I* disappeared.

It is easy to leave things behind, to deny there is a center to our lives, to avoid the substance of an inner existence that can either gnaw at our heart or close off the heart from caring. I thought, for a while, when I was younger, that I was the center of my own woods, that I could manage the universe with dexterity and aplomb, but now, in light of the simplest spider doing her work, looping threads of her web back and forth because it is her destiny, I can see in my own life that it is, simply, my part to be father, husband, writer, and old man in a young boy's heart who discovered a few things of beauty in those woods along the way, and I am glad.

May Sarton

The moon is reflecting light against my neighbor's window.

In 1987, Fred Rogers invited me to his children's television neighborhood. "Chris," he said, "I've also invited a poet. I thought it would be good for the children if they met two writers together talking about what they love to do."

"Who is the poet?" I asked.

"May Sarton, " Fred answered.

The first time I came across the name May Sarton was on the Op/Ed page of *The New York Times* in 1974. She had written an essay on solitude that was one of the most beautiful essays on the subject I had ever read. I clipped out the piece and filed it in my desk drawer. I used that essay many times when I was a high school English teacher. Thirteen years later I was sitting in Fred Rogers' office in television station WQED in Pittsburgh with May Sarton the poet, novelist, journal writer, dreamer, lover of cats, flowers, and the sea.

May was exhausted from her journey to Pittsburgh and was feeling uncomfortable, so I helped her into her chair, rearranged the cushions, helped prop up her legs. She smiled, looked down at me, and said, "You're a writer, too?"

At that time in my life I kept such a notion hidden from everyone, mostly from myself, for to admit that one is a writer is to admit that one is either a fool or a visionary. I didn't want to be a fool, and I knew that I was not a visionary. "I just spend most of my free time writing," I said. May smiled again.

May and I were together with Fred on the children's program, a true visit, for being with Fred is being in the presence of a wise, bright, good man who serves God. When we travel to be in the presence of those we love or those who understand the true qualities of love and faith, such a journey becomes a true visit. Being in the presence of Fred Rogers is truly having a visit with a neighbor in God's community.

May and I kept in contact with each other ever since our first meeting in Pittsburgh. We wrote many, many letters back and forth, shared our victories and defeats. Once a year I drove to York, Maine, and slept in May's house that faced the Atlantic Ocean.

On one visit, May cooked me my first fresh lobster. She taught me how to crack open the shell and scoop out the good parts. Another time we had lunch at a small restaurant in town. On our way home she pointed out her favorite places along the road: a collection of wildflowers, the home of a friend, the trees that collect snow in a certain way in winter.

One of my favorite memories of my various visits with May was our reading poetry together on her couch. I would read one of my newest poems, and May would follow along with the sheet that I held up before us. After the poem, she would point out with her finger what she liked and didn't like in the work. When she liked the entire piece, she looked up at me and smiled. Then she would read some poems from her books.

Each Christmas, May sent me one of her famous Christmas cards, written in the summer, printed on special paper and with special ink in the fall. May wrote so often how much she loved to send out those Christmas cards.

Writers need writers, for it is among the community of those who struggle with the same tiger that there can be found solace when the beast attempts to devour us.

In the spring of 1995, May wrote that she was ill, sick in a different way, unable to write her poetry, unable to tend to her garden, unable to sustain the energy she once held over the common day. When a friend is ill, most of us would run to his side. I run the other way. This is one of my many flaws. But flowers. May loves flowers. *I'll send her flowers*, I thought, in the spring of 1995.

May was born in Belgium. Her mother's birthday was August third. My mother and father were both born in Belgium. My birthday is August third. May loved to tell me about the memories she had of that little country. Many of her memories were the same memories I had heard from my mother: the cities, the food, the songs and neighborhoods. May wrote in a letter, "We have so many bonds, and not the least is your Belgian heritage. Someday you and Roe and the children must go there and feel the wind and look at the extraordinary skies and maybe float on a canal for a few days."

I was going to send flowers to May. Year after year, month after month, May Sarton was a part of my life, a part of my writing, a person who stepped into my life with her letters, her encouragement, her kind words, her suggestions for improving a poem or an essay. I was going to send her flowers.

May seeped into my life, between the cracks of my walls that I had so carefully built. Flowers. I intended to send flowers to May, but she was ill, she was dying, she was in Maine, far away beside the unforgiving sea, among the weeds that grew in the garden she loved. May, I was going to send flowers to May Sarton the writer, my friend.

On Tuesday, July 18, 1995, I was casually reading *The New York Times.* Section B page one. Section B page four. Section B page six. Section ... section ... section B page seven: "May Sarton, Poet, Novelist and Individualist, Dies at 83."

I tore the obituary out of the paper and brought it to Roe. As she was reading, I just said, simply, "I *was* going to send her flowers."

I rearrange the world around me when I am faced with pain. I clean my desk, write a letter, or poem or essay. When my father had a stroke, I pretended he was another man. When my grandmother died, I dismissed it as a newspaper account of an old woman who lives so far away that she was out of my life most of the time, so what difference did it make if she died? Belgium was like heaven to me when I was a child: distant, filled with wonderful people and places my parents described. My grandmother in heaven, and my grandmother in Belgium. Same thing.

I have my house. My three children are sleeping in their beds as I write. Roe is sleeping. The cat and the dog are sleeping. The goldfish is moving back and forth in its bowl. It is dark outside. I see the reflection of the moon on my neighbor's window.

Either life is a false tableau made of ice and snow slowly melting each time the earth completes a rotation around the sun, or life is an accumulation of days and hours, a collection of moving parts and memories, preparing the soul for the final and infinite preservation with God.

I am afraid. Slowly, slowly people that I love are dying. I cannot stop the intrusion from seeping in. So I write:

To a Child Early at His Death

Rise, child, and bring dark earth with you
That grave blood knew and sweetness pressed
Out from your bones.

Join me here at this meal. My plate is empty.
Spread out your arms; cast off a shadow
In the shape of wings or dust.

I am the eyes to explain the cloud.
I am the keeper of this new distance
You have placed between us.

I shall admire your new clothes, your
Tin pots and dried fruit, all from your
Travels.

Is there honey in death?
A need for shirts and sweaters? Are the
Hungry fed and the fed good for singing?

I would be interested in your telling,
The sound of your voice, the dialect
You have learned from dust and light combined.

Do you like my table I have prepared?
Do you know what the flowers bring?
I have made these arrangements to greet you.

I believe there is honey in heaven, and light, and a bountiful table God prepares for our arrival. And I believe the flowers I planned to send to May Sarton were already waiting for her.

Forgive me, May, for I am still afraid. Smile when you see Roe, the children, and me floating down the canals of Belgium.

It is dark outside, but the moon *is* reflecting light against my neighbor's window.

Easter Is the Sun

He who doubts from what he sees
Will never believe, do what you please.
If the sun and moon should doubt
They'd immediately go out.

William Blake (1757-1827)

When I was a teacher I could not reconcile my wish to help my students become reflective people with the knowledge that the more reflective we become the more open we are to sadness.

A contemplative life invites the shadows into our inner world, the world of the soul that is open to both what is good and to what is dark and destructive. We do build up armor against such ruinous forces by the accumulation of wisdom, but such wisdom comes with a price: the realization that perfection does not exist, that we have to make compromises, that we see more and more what could be and have to accept the reality of what is, for it is in such acceptance that we come to tie together who we are and who we wish to be, what we want and what we have, where we are and where we wish we could be.

As I look out my window I see the wind shaking the leaves. A crow, flying against the wind, hovers in mid-air over my neighbor's house, leaves roll down the street like children doing cartwheels. The force of winter recedes to the force of spring, fighting out the battle in my front yard. This resembles my own struggles as I too try to manage divergent seasons of myself.

I want to be a child still, and yet the world wants me to be an adult. I've done fairly well, married a woman who loves and tolerates me. We raised three good children who please us daily, I am juggling a career in education with a career in writing, but I also want to still be a child. I want to run outside in the wind with my sister Anne and pretend that we are caught in a hurricane as we did when she was ten and I was eight. I want to see how many goose eggs we can find in the swamp and mark the nest's location in my mind so that I can return in a few weeks and see the goslings.

Between winter and spring there is a sense that we are giving up something: the harsh cold to the smell of warm earth, the stark beauty of snow to the mud and rain. We need a season between the seasons, taking what is best, let's say, from winter and combining that with what is best from spring. How nice to pick daffodils in a snow covered field. How good to ice skate in seventy degree weather.

This past Easter I was reminded how far I've come from the days when I ran to a clump of grass hoping to find a chocolate egg wrapped in silver as my father pointed with his finger to a spot just to the right.

My mother is seventy-five years old. My father is eighty-five years old. On Easter my brother Bruno and my sister-in-law Lori and their son Marc and his fiancee Christa stood around the dining room table along with my sister Anne and my brother-in-law John and their sons Matthew, Dan, and Michael, along with my other sister Maria and my brother-in-law Peter and their children Christopher and Sarah, my brother Jose, and my son David and my daughter Karen. We all stood around the Easter table as our friend, Fr. John Catoir, thanked God for the food, for the family, for the time together. My wife, Roe, was home with Michael. They were both sick with fevers, and they both insisted that David, Karen, and I ought not to miss Easter.

This was one of the few times that I was at a family function without Roe. She was out there somewhere. I was home with my brothers and sisters. When I arrived at the front door and hugged my sister Anne, I felt like asking, "Wanna go look for goose eggs?"

During the day, by brother Bruno spoke with great enthusiasm about his growing autograph collection. I felt like asking him, "Wanna go see our names that you scratched in the kitchen window thirty years ago?"

When my brother Jose spoke about completing his extraordinary book about exchange theory, I felt like asking him if he wanted to just go outside and pick some daffodils.

During the traditional Easter egg hunt, I watched my youngest niece, three-year-old Sarah, stoop and pick up chocolate eggs that my father hid in the grass. I was hoping that he would look at *me* and point to a certain clump of grass, but he didn't.

For a moment I stepped away from everyone as they made their way through the garden. I sat on a small rock wall my father built fifty years ago. I looked at my family, my brothers and sisters, their husbands and wives, the various children in various stages eating candy, laughing, talking. Then I realized that I am no different than I was when I was Sarah's age. I am still a three-year-old boy hunting in the grass for bits of delicious chocolate my father hid. I am still seventeen years old, throwing jelly beans at my sister's head as she makes her way past the apple tree. I am a forty-five-year-old man sitting on a wall as my thirteen-year-old daughter steps up and says "Come on lazy bones."

I looked at this young woman standing before me and I felt that wind rushing around me, that wind that keeps the crow up in mid-air, that wind that pushes the leaves. I felt my daughter's hand as she pulled me up from the wall, and I felt the best that spring has to offer: hope, warmth, the hair of a young girl bouncing on her shoulders as she stoops down, picks up a chocolate egg and hands it to her father. "Happy Easter, Daddy," Karen whispers, and suddenly I don't care that I am not three or seventeen. I am just content, filled with a deep sense of contemplation as I look at this girl, this woman, this daughter I call mine, but she is not mine. She belongs to spring and to the future and to all that waits for her. I looked at my eighty-five-year-old father and thought, "What must he think as he sits on the wall and considers the day?"

After the Easter egg hunt, I called Roe to see how she was doing. I woke her up.

"That's okay. I had to get up anyway. I was reading on the couch and I just fell asleep. Michael and I are fine. Are you having a good time?"

It was impossible to speak over the phone about the twenty years we have spent together. It was impossible to speak about the chocolate eggs. It was impossible to explain to Roe that I saw a glimpse of paradise, but I did say this in response to her question: "Yes, I am having a very nice time, and I am so glad to hear your voice. I'll be home soon."

"Don't rush. Stay as long as you like. Michael and I are going to have a bit of dinner. We're not very hungry, then we're going to watch some television."

"Okay. I love you."

"I love you too. See you in a while."

I hung up the phone and walked into the living room of my youth, sat on the couch between my brother and sister. My father adjusted his hearing aid. My mother passed around some recent photographs. I ate a chocolate egg and felt just fine, not sad, not happy, just content, reflective, a bit cautious, older, with my soul intact held together with the hand of my daughter, the voices of my wife and sons, the images of my brothers and sisters, the memory of my father as a young man stooping over next to me in the garden as he whispers, "There's a marshmallow rabbit under that pile of leaves."

What a garden it was; what a garden it is, the garden of Eden, the garden of paradise, the garden of my youth, the garden of memory. What we take out from such a place and what we add determines the condition of our souls. I think my soul is made of chocolate.

Home

The Lord watches over you—
the Lord is your shade at your right hand;
the sun will not harm you by day,
nor the moon by night.
The Lord will keep you from all harm—
he will watch over your life;
the Lord will watch over your coming and going
both now and forevermore.

Psalm 121:5–8

When Roe and I bought our house from an old couple who had no children, we both felt an immediate connection to the yard. Although the space was small, it nurtured ten large oak trees four or five stories tall. The previous owners surrounded the base of each tree with periwinkle. In the middle of the yard a concrete birdbath stood up with its open bowl of dignity and generosity.

I've planted grass seeds eighteen times, fertilized intermittently, attacked grubs, built a shed, erected two swing sets, and built one sandbox. After ten years Roe and I hired a builder to construct an addition to the house. Five years later we hired someone else to assemble a deck. With each new construction, we cut into our small track of land.

I read somewhere that the only man-made structure astronauts can see as they circle the globe is the Great Wall of China. No one will notice our shed or the wide deck.

In the southwestern corner of the yard is a small, sturdy clay pot. When my first son, David, was four years old, I carried this pot from the garage, turned it upside down and placed it in the corner under the mock orange bush. I called this a secret place, and for years David liked to run to that small seat and hide under the bush. The pot is still there. David is now seventeen years old.

One winter the birdbath cracked. Roe and I placed the base and broken bowl on the curb for the trash collection.

Sometimes, usually in the summer, when the moon is full, I walk out into the yard, sit on the grass and look up between the tree branches, and frame the moon between the open leaves. That is all. I just sit and look. I pat the ground sometimes. Often our dog emerges from the darkness and sits beside me. Sometimes I take off my shoes and socks. A useless gesture.

A man I worked with for a number of years, who was in his late fifties said, as we walked toward our cars, "Yep. Kids are gone. The dog's dead." He laughed, then closed the top button of his winter coat. It was snowing.

Is there such a thing as virgin forest in America? I don't think so. Have we taken up all the space available? Is there any piece of land that does not belong to someone? We make our claims. We work the land. We scratch in the dirt.

The children have trampled all the periwinkle into dust during their games of running bases or mother-may-I, or baseball.

I've buried six goldfish under the rhododendron, four mice, a chipmunk, a robin. The children have slept in the tent out back, practiced catching, conquered the territory with their water balloons. They have eaten hamburgers and watermelons during summer afternoon barbecues; they have dodged each others' snowballs. The septic tank was rebuilt once and emptied four times.

It is mid-January as I write. For some reason the temperature jumped to fifty-five degrees today. The floodlight is on. As I look out my window, I see a single moth dancing in the light. January moth. January light. Old, dirty snow covers the backyard.

One year Roe and I planted raspberries in the northwestern portion of the yard. I remember in late October how pleased I was to find a single raspberry. I picked the bit of fruit and squeezed it between my tongue and the roof of my mouth. A last piece of summer savored in October. The raspberries began to encroach on the neighbor's property and on everything else it seemed, so I pulled up the plants and dragged them to the town compost dump.

The swing sets are gone. The sandbox is gone. David is seventeen. Karen is fourteen. Michael is twelve. Our dog is four years old. I know it is all here, the future memories.

I sit on the grass in the darkness and feel the plain earth. Dust to dust and I must linger with finite time with my growing children. Dust to dust and I find my way back to the first day when Roe and I bought our little house and land where the days were young and the moon spoke out with optimism and hope.

Someday I will be like my former colleague and lament the death of our dog and the fact that the children have grown and taken off for their own plot of ground to plant and nurture. At times I already feel like the January moth, throwing myself against the false summer light that once was bright and warm and real and filled with the sounds of my children laughing.

Someday Roe and I will drive the car out to the garden center, drive home and surround each tree in the lawn with periwinkle. We'll buy another cement birdbath, and then we will hammer a FOR SALE sign into the generous earth of the front lawn.

Survival and Love

The moon like a flower
In heaven's high bower
With silent delights
Sits and smiles on the night.

William Blake

All that matters, matters in death for it is then that the harvest is complete, and what the barn yields for a future hunger depends upon what has been kept. I am a keeper of words: hoeing, planting, adding moisture, pulling up the weeds that surround the small, green plant of what I wish to compose.

For twenty-two years I have been writing poems and essays, gathering them in my files, sending them out to editors, accumulating acceptances and rejections from the marketplace, and that has been good. But there is more to being a writer than publication. I wish to provide sustenance when there is little to eat. Some writers wish to fill the void of boredom in the reader, so the writer entertains. Some writers wish to inform people, so they become journalists. There are writers who write simply for money, so they write what they know will sell for the moment, gossip mostly.

True writing is, as Ezra Pound once said, "news that stays news." What is common to us today and what is common to a person six thousand years ago and what is common to the people of a long, distant future ... these are the things of art. A writer who develops a certain longing in his or her reader, or a certain attitude of power and remorse, or joy and fatigue, this is a writer who survives, for this is the writer who continues to feed a reader's divine self: the soul, the laughter, the part of ourselves that seeks wheat and water.

We choose to survive. We wish to survive. We seek respite from illness. We seek favors from death: a reprieve, a long delay.

We continue to wake up in the morning with hope and with renewed energy. It is this hope and energy that people seek in a writer's work, or in the type of work I strive to create. At least I know that what I leave in my folders will someday be read by my children. They will be able to see a bit of what it is I had hoped to pass along to them: beauty in the shadow of ugliness, courage in the jaws of fear, faith before the idols, justice shackled to the desperate arms of human nature.

This past weekend Roe and I drove to Bennington, Vermont. We hadn't taken a trip alone for many years. David is mature, responsible, and a free sitter for the younger children, though now Karen and Michael would resent my saying that they need a baby-sitter. It is the wrong use of words to define what it is they need when Roe and I leave the house. The children need protection, and David is now at the age where he can provide that protection for his brother and sister (along with the help and surveillance of three neighbors).

We were to stay with friends just east of Manchester, but along the way, Roe and I decided to stop at various craft and antique stores in Bennington. We bought a clay bowl with brown speckles, maple syrup, and a brass bucket.

As we pulled into Route 9 again, leaving the store behind us, we passed the beautiful Bennington Four Chimneys Inn to our left, drove down a small hill and came upon a beautiful country church. "I think Robert Frost is buried behind this church," I said as Roe opened a Vermont visitor's guide she had received from a friend the day before. She flipped through a few pages, and then read aloud: "Old First Church, Bennington, built in 1806. The graveyard dates to the Revolutionary War and also contains the grave of poet Robert Frost."

The fact that it was raining didn't deter my initial idea. "I'd like to see his grave." Roe looked out the windshield between the fast-moving wipers and the gush of water.

"I have an umbrella in the suitcase," she said as she reached to the back seat, unzipped the case, and pulled out one of those mini, compact, collapsible umbrellas fit for a mouse. We both laughed as the church wobbled in front of us through the water splashing against the car. "I'm willing," she said.

I drove the car to the right side of the church, parked, turned the engine off, and buried my dry body into my winter coat.

As Roe and I stepped out from the car, we noticed that the rain had suddenly stopped and turned into a slow drizzle, but the wind inverted Roe's umbrella, and she laughed and laughed. We held hands, walked up to the front of the church, looked inside the windows, and walked around to the entrance of the cemetery.

"I wonder how we're going to find his grave," I said with an automatic tone of defeat as I looked across at the hundreds of tombstones that stood before us like an odd collection of the Ten Commandments.

Roe pulled my hand. "I guess we'll just have to follow the sign," she said as she pointed to a green piece of wood with yellow letters: *Robert Frost Grave.*

We followed other small green signs with small yellow arrows through the winding road of the cemetery. We both wondered if his gravesite would be simple, or pretentious.

Arrow. Arrow. Down a small hill. Arrow. To the right. Arrow. And there it was, a long, rectangular slab of gray stone the size of a kitchen table, a simple stone decorated with simple carved leaves that formed the border, and engraved were the names of the poet and his family. Under Robert Frost's name was a line from one of his poems: "I had a lover's quarrel with the world."

I snapped a picture of the tombstone, then Roe suggested that she take a picture of me looking down at the grave marker. "I don't know if it will come out. It's so dark."

I in my hooded coat leaned forward a bit as I tried to read the carved words again, and then I was overcome with grief and felt a bit what Scrooge might have felt as he looked down at his own tombstone as the ghost of Christmas Future pointed his bony finger. I am no Frost, nor was meant to be, nor will I ever achieve the taunting beauty he created, though I still felt one with the dead poet as I looked down, a bit perplexed. *So this is where the body goes after the writing of the poems,* I thought, then Roe clicked the camera.

In school I disliked the poems of Frost because they seemed foreign, school-like, and they were to me at the time incomprehensible. I had my fill of incomprehensible things when I was a schoolboy, and I didn't need Robert Frost to add to the confusion. Yet, many years later, after discovering for myself the beauty that waits like hidden raspberries under protective leaves, I drank the juice of poetry, sucked the fruit, returned to the harvest again and again for more, and such a harvest included the poems of Frost, for it was from Frost that I learned the lesson of casting out into the unknown, what it feels like out there, and the comfort of knowing that just beyond the hayfield the still and solemn house patiently waited for my sure return.

When Roe and I returned to the children the next evening, they embraced us, caught us up on all the news, then Michael said, ten minutes later, "It feels as if you never left." He leaped over the dog and disappeared into the living room, with the dog chasing close behind.

When we return to the writers we love, we, too, feel that inner peace and can also say, "It feels as if you never left me," for it is in the mixture of true writing that the reader discovers a security and a familiar place that offers true solace. I believe that true art offers us a glimpse of heaven in the soft color of moonlight.

"I hope the pictures turn out," Roe said that night as we prepared for bed. "They will," I said as I kissed her good night.

All in time, in time, the pictures will turn out in glorious color as long as we plant, harvest, and store up our lives for the time when we are hungry, for it is at that time that we will be saved. In the meantime, yes, let us continue to have a lover's quarrel with the world: survival and love, survival and love, all our efforts are spent on survival and love.

Old Woman
at the Nursing Home

I would like to know the evening.
Can you give me the evening
From dusk to the first lamp light,
Yellow and tea perhaps, or a rosary
To count time away with prayer?

Can you give what is not given:
Order? An arrangement of stars?

I would like an arrangement of stars
In a circle, a crown for my head.

I am here with my dress
Spread out around me: printed flowers,
Violets: purple and blue.

I once knew the names of
All the constellations.

Moon, moon, push the broom;
Sweep the evening clean.

Have you seen my children?
I would like to know their names again
One by one stitched inside my dress.
Are they against the darkness
In some pattern?

I would like to know the moon—moon,
Push the broom.

The moon is made of green cheese.

John Heywood (1497–1580)

Look for these books
by Christopher de Vinck

The Power of the Powerless
This is Christopher de Vinck's true account
of his severely handicapped brother's life—
a powerful, inspirational statement on the
value of life.
Softcover: 0-310-48691-2

Simple Wonders
The Disarming Pleasure
of Looking Beyond the Seen
With his gifted writing style, de Vinck un-
covers the truth and beauty in the ordinary
in this book of daily meditations.
Hardcover: 0-310-49891-0

Threads of Paradise
In the Fabric of Everyday Life
A follow-up to *Simple Wonders*, this book
gives a different perspective on life, again
helping us discover the truth and beauty in
our ordinary, everyday lives.
Hardcover: 0-310-49931-3

ZondervanPublishingHouse
Grand Rapids, Michigan 49530
http://www.zondervan.com

We want to hear from you. Please send your comments about
this book to us in care of the address below. Thank you.

ZondervanPublishingHouse
Grand Rapids, Michigan 49530
http://www.zondervan.com